COUNSELING
THE
UNWED MOTHER

SUCCESSFUL PASTORAL COUNSELING SERIES

COUNSELING
THE
UNWED MOTHER

HELEN E. TERKELSEN

PRENTICE-HALL, INC., ENGLEWOOD CLIFFS, N.J.

Counseling the Unwed Mother
by Helen E. Terkelsen

© 1964 by Prentice-Hall, Inc.,
Englewood Cliffs, New Jersey

Library of Congress Catalog Card Number: 64–20746

Printed in the United States of America
T 20746

PRENTICE-HALL INTERNATIONAL, INC., *London*
PRENTICE-HALL OF AUSTRALIA, PTY., LTD., *Sydney*
PRENTICE-HALL OF CANADA, LTD., *Toronto*
PRENTICE-HALL OF INDIA (PRIVATE) LTD., *New Delhi*
PRENTICE-HALL OF JAPAN, INC., *Tokyo*
PRENTICE-HALL DE MEXICO, S.A., *Mexico City*

The PASTOR'S PRAYER

O God, whose glory shines round about those who worship thee, who opens our eyes by thy Grace to the wonders of thy kingdom, guide us that we may awaken those who are asleep to thee through their own misfortunes that thy glory may dawn upon them and they may come alive again. Help us to use the gifts that have been placed in our hands and upon our hearts to lighten the burdens of those who are searching so desperately for the gift of love that they accept substitutes not of thy spirit. As we devote our thoughts and hearts, O God, to understanding and helping the young woman who bears her child outside of the family circle, let us witness to the sanctification of family life and the dignity of all motherhood. As thou hast charged us with this work, Our Father, give us the understanding, the patience, and the heart to perform it well in the name of Christ, our Master Teacher. Amen.

INTRODUCTION

This series of books represents the most comprehensive publishing effort ever made in the field of pastoral care. These books could not have been published twenty-five years ago or probably even ten, for the material was not then available. In the past, single books have been available covering different phases of the task. Now we are bringing the subjects together in a single series. Here we present a library of pastoral care covering the major topics and problems that most pastors will encounter in their ministry. Fortunately, not all of these problems need be faced every week or even every month. But, when they are, the minister wants help and he wants it immediately.

These books are prepared for the nonspecialized minister serving the local church, where he is the most accessible professional person in the community. It is a well-accepted fact that more people turn to clergy when in trouble than to all other professional people. Therefore, the pastor must not fail them.

Russell L. Dicks
General Editor

FOREWORD

Hardly a more poignant crisis arises for the young woman than a pregnancy out of wedlock. Yet those to whom such a woman turns for help frequently are unsure how to advise. Their uncertainty arises to a large extent from the complexity of the problem which involves prenatal, medical, and emotional care of the mother, a realistic plan for the infant, and financial, legal and emotional involvement of the alleged father. The situation may be further complicated by the families of the couple, the social climate of the community, and the availability of legal or social resources.

The religious counselor is frequently in the unique position of offering the first constructive steps in mobilizing emotional and social resources. For unlike others who are in the position of potential service, he is already a trusted ally of the girl and her family. By virtue of his position in the community, he is expected to know how to handle delicate matters, but all too often he may feel inadequate to the specific challenge of dealing with illegitimacy.

Mrs. Terkelsen's work should come as a welcome "primer" for those religious counselors who cope with this social problem. She presents with clarity the social, religious and psychological aspects of the unwed mother in a way which I am sure will be most useful to the clergy. All of us who work extensively in the field of emotional counseling, whether it be social work, psychology, psychiatry, or the ministry, must utilize all of our resources individually and collectively to be of real value to those we serve. None can use our help more than the unwed mother.

Bernard L. Busfield, Jr., M.D.

Psychiatric Consultant
Crittenton Hastings House
Boston, Mass.

Staff Psychiatrist
Massachusetts Mental Health Center
Boston, Mass.

CONTENTS

Part I

THE PROBLEM OF THE UNWED MOTHER

Part II

THE BACKGROUND AND DYNAMICS OF THE UNWED MOTHER

Part III

THE COUNSELING PROCESS

PREFACE

While the clergyman has been concerned with the unwed mother and her problem as well as the problems her situation creates ever since the first young woman in such trouble came to him, he has not been aware until recently that he was not dealing with isolated cases. Then he began to read in newspapers, periodicals and professional journals that this was becoming a major problem in our society. Other professions were making studies of the young women pregnant out of wedlock in order to cope more effectively with the problem. The pastoral counselor could read the literature of social work, psychology, medicine and law but there was little help for him there. He is a pastor, one member of the team of trained and dedicated people whose concern is the welfare of others. It is primarily for him that this book is written. If it should prove useful to others, I would be grateful.

The Staff and the Board of Trustees of Crittenton Hastings House have given their whole-hearted endorsement to this work. I especially thank Dr. Bernard L. Busfield, Jr. and Dr. David W. Haughey for their guidance in the preparation of the chapters dealing with the psychological material.

I must express my appreciation to the many people who have shown an interest in this work and have offered help in whatever way I could use it. I am deeply grateful to my good friend and neighbor, Mrs. David L. Campbell, for the hours of work she spent so cheerfully and promptly typing the manuscript and its many revisions; to my son Andrew whose checking the manuscript prompted those revisions; and to my dear husband who endured much that this book—which he suggested long before it was undertaken—might be written.

Part I

THE PROBLEM OF THE UNWED MOTHER

CHAPTER ONE

The EXTENT Of The PROBLEM

"My mother said that having a baby when you aren't married and then getting rid of it is the worst sin there is."

"What do you mean, getting rid of it?"

"Well, placing it for adoption."

"You mean she thinks you should keep your baby?"

"She says that getting married to the baby's father is the only way. Then the baby has a name and the sin can be forgiven. I don't believe a bad marriage is good even under these circumstances. I made one mistake in getting pregnant, but it would be worse to marry a person like him. I just won't, and my mother says I've got to. So now I'm guilty of two unforgivable sins—adultery, or whatever you call it, and dishonoring my parents by not doing what they say . . . disobeying them."

"You feel God can't forgive these sins?"

"Oh, I know, God forgives if you are repentant. At least, that's what the church says. But I don't feel forgiven. Besides, how can he forgive me if I refuse to make it right by not marrying and by disobeying my parents? That's why I haven't been going to church. I don't feel I have any right to."

This girl had not talked with her local pastor because her mother could not bear the shame of having him know their terrible secret. Fortunately, this attitude is not so prevalent as it once was, since more people are aware that their ministers are approachable in crises of this kind. Furthermore, Jerry's mother did not think that her minister had knowledge of how her daughter might cope with her situation, nor did she know how many girls every year have gone first to their pastor for help. It is to increase his resources in this matter that this book is presented to the pastoral counselor.

Jerry, 22 years old, a member of an established Protestant church, attractive and intelligent, held a good job until she entered the maternity home. She was one of nearly 245,000 young women in the United States who in 1962, bore their babies out of wedlock.[1] Despite a general impression that the teen-age group has the highest percentage of illegitimate babies, it is Jerry's age group in which this occurs most frequently. Hannah M. Adams and Ursula M. Gallagher of the Children's Bureau of the United States Department of Health, Education and Welfare explain this as follows:[2] The actual number of births to unmarried teen-age girls rose from 51,700 in 1945 to 91,700 in 1960; this represents an increase in rate of out-of-wedlock births from 9.5 to 15.7 per thousand for these younger girls. The rate has stayed about the same since 1955. At the present time, the annual illegitimacy rate is about 15 per thousand among this younger group and about 40 per thousand among unmarried women 20 to 30 years of age.

The increase in fertility of all women was from a rate of 86 births per thousand in 1945 to 120 births per thousand in 1959. During this same period, illegitimate births rose from a rate of 10 to 22 per thousand.[3] These rates of increase are included to answer the frequently asked question of whether or not the increase in illegitimate births is explained by a general increase in birth rate as well as by better methods of recording all births. While these figures are important, it should be recognized that the problems arising from out-of-wedlock births are not caused by the increase. It is unfortunate that we must first be alarmed by crises proclaimed by headlines before we allow ourselves to become aware of a continuing problem that demands our attention if we are to understand it. Even when we learn that the out-of-wedlock pregnancy of teen-age girls is not increasing, we should not be lulled into a false sense of security.

The statistics used in this chapter are as reliable as it is possible to make them, but one must keep in mind that there can be only esti-

---

[1] U.S. Department of Health, Education and Welfare. Public Health Service, National Vital Statistics Division. Annual vital statistics of the U.S.

[2] Hannah M. Adams and Ursula M. Gallagher, "Some Facts and Observations about Illegitimacy," *Children*, Vol. 10, No. 2, March–April, 1963, pp. 43–44.

[3] *Ibid.*, p. 43.

mates for the fifteen states which omit information about legitimacy on birth certificates. Furthermore, not included in these figures are the babies born to women made pregnant by men other than their husbands. These births appear as legal on the record. One must also remember that these statistics are based on the number of babies born out of wedlock; they have scant relation to babies conceived out of wedlock.

The pastor should also be as concerned with the increasing practice of abortion to solve this problem, for it is a solution to the problem that is commonly used, especially by middle-class and upper-class girls. The alternative choice of marriage is another possibility that the pastor must consider. Although he probably does not keep a record of the fact, he is aware of the number of big, healthy babies born too soon after marriage to be considered premature. While the practical problem of these three groups of unmarried pregnant girls (those who have an abortion, those who marry hastily, and those who become unwed mothers) are different, the concern of the pastor for their future welfare is the same in each case.

In 1960, the total number of out-of-wedlock births was estimated to be 224,300. Of these, 37 percent was to white mothers and 63 percent to nonwhite mothers.[4] It has been suggested by the United States Bureau of Health, Education and Welfare, as well as other government and private agencies, that in areas where lack of education, few employment opportunities, poor housing, inadequate recreation, and low income prevail there is a higher incidence of out-of-wedlock pregnancy. Obviously, however, favorable environment is no guarantee that the situation will not arise. The unwed mother is to be found in all strata of society and in all the subcultures of this country. As a rule no pastor encounters unwed mothers from all levels of society, because his parish will more probably embrace a limited segment of the social strata. Yet the unwed mother who asks for his help must be seen by him, not only as an individual in trouble, but as a troubled individual in a given social context. It is this viewpoint that may provide a clue not only to the cause of her predicament but to the solution as well.

---

[4] *Ibid.*, p. 43.

People concerned with the extent of the problem—or problems—of out-of-wedlock births frequently have preconceived notions about the way the children of these mothers are cared for. Too often some city or state dwellers, dissatisfied with their welfare departments, will point an accusing finger at the illegitimately born children in the community and say, "That's the cause of all the trouble." Statistically, such accusation is not proved. In a report issued in 1960, the Bureau of Family Services (then the Bureau of Public Assistance) of the Department of Health, Education and Welfare estimated that 2.5 million children in the United States under eighteen years of age had been born out of wedlock. Of these, only 13 percent were receiving aid as dependent children in November, 1958.[5]

In Boston a few years ago, there was a furor over the Aid to Dependent Children program. Its detractors claimed it encouraged illegitimacy. At that time, of all the children cared for in this way, only 25 percent were illegitimate, and the number born to mothers who were already receiving aid was relatively low. The actual amount received is seldom an incentive of itself to propagate illegitimacy. One report indicated that almost 40 percent of the unwed mothers find other means of support within a year, and 20 percent within six months.[6] To be sure, there are enough flamboyant abuses to arouse the public when these are aired in the daily press. But then, one robbery doesn't precipitate a city-wide curfew today. Rather the offender is dealt with individually.

Nothing has been mentioned and little will be throughout the rest of this book about the numbers of unwed fathers. There simply are no statistics. Often the mother does not know the whereabouts of the father. The liaison may have been a casual one, and the man or boy may be ignorant of the mother's pregnancy. Then, too, the man may flee so that he will not be held morally and financially responsible for his act. In some circumstances, he may flee to avoid being jailed for statutory rape. His name, if known, does not appear on the birth certificate. There are agencies that are having some degree of

5 "Illegitimacy and Its Impact on the Aid to Dependent Children Program," Bureau of Public Assistance, p. 35.
6 "A.D.C. Fact Sheet," Boston Welfare Department (1959).

success in communicating with the unwed male parents, but by and large the men and boys avoid the agencies and the counselors.[7] Sometimes these elusive fathers present other problems: it has happened that two residents in a maternity home, upon comparing their stories in detail (which they are urged not to do for obvious reasons) found that the same young man-about-town was the father of both of their babies. It has also been revealed that one man has mated previously and/or subsequently without benefit of marriage. Such a man may be already married. These facts do not get into the statistics even if they are on the case records.

Of the close to 250,000 young women pregnant out of wedlock each year, only about one in ten use the facilities of the maternity homes throughout the country.

Consider these social and health service figures. "About one unmarried mother in six received service from a public or voluntary child welfare agency. The younger mothers were more likely to receive service than the older ones, almost one in three of those under fifteen years of age compared with one in seven of those past twenty years of age."[8]

"One day in 1961 there were about 6,500 girls and women with the problem of illegitimate pregnancy receiving service through state and local public child welfare programs. Fifty percent of these 6,500 unwed mothers were living with parents or relatives. Sixteen percent were in independent living arrangements, and 24 percent were in foster care—thirteen percent in foster homes and eleven percent in maternity homes. One-third were from families receiving assistance."[9]

Often when this tragedy of pregnancy without marriage comes to a family, it feels that it is alone against a hostile world, even though its members may have sympathized with the plight of unwed mothers in magazine articles and television programs. It is fiction until it hits home; then it is a nightmare! Just as the naive girl says, "It's nobody's business what I do with my sex life," so her family thinks it's nobody's business what skeletons it keeps in its closets.

---

[7] See Reuben Pannor's article, "Casework Service for Unmarried Fathers," *Children,* Vol. 10, No. 2, March–April, 1963, pp. 65–70.

[8] Adams and Gallagher, *op. cit.,* p. 45.

[9] *Ibid.,* pp. 45–46.

Statistics show that many have made it their business—not out of curiosity or malice, but to be able to help when called upon.

What becomes of all the babies? Are they all adopted? How can the girls keep them? About thirty percent of all the illegitimately born babies (approximately seventy percent of white and five percent of nonwhite illegitimate babies) are released for adoption. The other seventy percent born out of wedlock are raised by their mothers, by people chosen by the mother—sometimes by women who are strangers to her and whose sole qualification is that they are available—or in agency foster homes and institutions. Among the mothers who receive maternity-home care, the figures approximate 75 percent of the children adopted and 25 percent not adopted.[10] In 1961, it is estimated that 66,100 adoption petitions were filed for children born illegitimately. Of this number, only ten percent were for nonwhite babies even though 63 percent of all illegitimate babies are nonwhite.

The decision to give up a baby born out of wedlock is often reached only after a period of intense emotional conflict within the mother, and statistics offer little comfort to the mother caught between the demands of conscience and practicality. Often the cultural and economic background of the mother decisively influences the decision reached. Yet, the battle must be fought alone by each mother in such desperate circumstances. Only the outcome of the battle is reflected in the above statistics.

There is a precedent for every solution and every attempt at solution of the problems of the unwed mother. Statistics can be found to prove almost anything one wishes to prove. The truth remains that too many young women are pregnant out of wedlock, and they need our help. In many cases, it is the parish minister who has the first opportunity to give this help. It behooves him to use every skill and tool at his command.

Frequently, the unwed mother consults the nearest minister not for spiritual direction, but for practical help. She wants his support for her half-made plan. She may turn to him for help, because she thinks her story is safer with him than with the local family service agency. This is not necessarily true. Not infrequently, she presents

---

[10] *Ibid.*, p. 46.

the pastoral counselor with a problem that might be handled more adequately by the social agency. There is need for cooperation between the two professions so that one does not assume the functions and roles of the other. The pastoral counselor should not undertake the work of the adoption agency, the attorney, the physician, the psychiatrist, the school principal or the judge. The Christian minister is the shepherd of his flock, a follower of him who forgave much because he loved much, who forgave the adulterer just as surely as he forgave other sinners. The love of Jesus was great enough so that his words, "Go in peace," provided people with the incentive to undertake a new life, free from past sins.

The pastor who wishes to cooperate with the other helping professions will first reassure the distraught young woman that he will help her. He will assure her that it is not the end of the world, and that practical plans can be made with the help of those more experienced in such matters. Later, they can discuss some of the more disturbing factors associated with the pregnancy: for example, the emotions of the girl, and the troubled personal relations.

There are a number of ways of handling out-of-wedlock pregnancies. Some may be acceptable to the pastoral counselor while others remain unacceptable to most ministers because they create more problems than solutions. The current practices are:

1. Marriage either to the father of the baby or to another man aware of the girl's condition, but willing to assume responsibility for both the mother and child.
2. Abortion either illegally in the U.S. or legally outside the U.S.
3. Precipitating a physical emergency for the purpose of being admitted to the local hospital for immediate treatment.
4. Keeping the baby following delivery in the local hospital; then, either taking it home to be raised as the child of the grandparents, maintaining him with welfare help, or working to support him and pay for day care.
5. Leaving home to have the baby anonymously in a large city and then releasing it for adoption.
6. Going to a maternity home for prenatal care and delivery and then placing the baby in the care of a qualified social agency for subsequent adoption.

Note: There are also combinations and variations of these practices.

It is natural for the pastor to react to some of the methods favorably and to others with grim disfavor. None of these methods, however, is good in itself if it is not well managed. Where there is understanding, warmth, and acceptance, no method is a total loss or an unmitigated evil. Unfortunately, the greatest area of neglect is in prenatal care. Rose Bernstein, a social worker who has done much work and study in this field, says, "Prenatal care should receive priority attention in considering the needs of unmarried mothers because of the relatively higher incidence of prematurity, fetal and perinatal deaths, complications of pregnancy, and maternal mortality associated with inadequate care."[11]

---

[11] Rose Bernstein, "Gaps in Services to Unmarried Mothers," *Children,* Vol. 10, No. 2 (March–April, 1963), p. 49.

CHAPTER TWO

ATTITUDES TOWARD OUT-Of-WEDLOCK
PREGNANCY

Most of the older segment of the population of the United States today still carries traces of an odd mixture of Puritanism and Romanticism that is a heritage of the Victorian age. Those were the days when a good wife called her husband Mr. Jones, not John, when night clothes and beach clothes were as voluminous as tea gowns. It was when a peek at a lady's ankle was more exciting than an extensive view of the natural beauty above a low-cut dress. It was when Mrs. Jones, if she knew about it at all, made no comments on her husband's excursions into the rowdy parts of town where the lights burned lower and later than they did at home.

It was at this time when a few brave and concerned men and women began to do something to help the number of unwed mothers in the large industrialized cities to which they came from the country to get jobs in factories, hotels, and large domestic establishments. When these newly arrived girls became pregnant out of wedlock in the course of learning how to get along in the big city, they were regarded as pariahs whom no "nice" person could accept as worthy of help. (Even social welfare in those days was only for the worthy poor.) Charles Crittenton was a concerned person who began his work in New York in 1885 after a personal misfortune that caused him to reevaluate his way of life and his purpose in it. He became an evangelist. Later he joined his efforts to those of a woman, Dr. Kate Waller Barrett, who first began to help unmarried mothers in Atlanta, Georgia, where her husband was an Episcopal clergyman. In New England in 1836, the Boston Female Reform Society was established to help girls who had "gone wrong" either because they

had been "taken advantage of" or because they "had weak characters." The accent was on *reform* in all these early efforts. While the
Protestant church was not represented per se in these efforts it
should be noted that it was men and women of religious leanings,
often clergymen, who supported and advanced this work. The
Roman Catholic Church, through its charitable agencies and institutions, and the Salvation Army, through its general rehabilitation
program, were also pioneers in the work.

This early work was geared to helping the mother successfully
through pregnancy and delivery and at the same time preparing her
to earn her living in a decent, usually domestic, way so that she
could care for her child properly. Adoption was not regarded as a
solution to the unwed mother's problem in those days because not
many people wanted to take a chance on a baby whose "bad blood"
might show up when it got to a "certain age." These mothers and
their children were a problem and an embarrassment to a society
which would rather not look at its double standards. But with social
services and social welfare replacing reform societies and charitable
agencies, and with the unwed mother coming from a different background altogether, the stereotype was changing along with the services available to her. There was also another important change: i.e.,
people were adopting many of the illegitimate offspring of the "girl-
next-door" type of unwed mother. Yet, as mentioned earlier, there is
still confusion of attitudes toward unmarried mothers, illicit coition,
and the babies whose origins are so inauspicious.

Before the first World War and the subsequent Roaring Twenties,
men had their pre- and extramarital experiences on the other side of
the tracks and in the red-light districts of the larger cities. It is no
longer necessary to go so far afield. Today the girl next door, the
wife in the next apartment in the housing project, and the steno in
the secretarial pool may be available if they are made to feel that
they are "loved" for their charm and glamour, that they can't be
resisted, and that the attentions of the propositioning gentleman are
honorable if not serious. That kind of *honorable* is hard to define
except to say that it implies that there is no intention to hurt or de-
grade. In the plush but not polished circles, a man has his choice of
the beautiful movie star—she may get a "quickie" divorce and demand

marriage, but that is no stumbling block—or of an old millionaire's young wife, or of a very expensive and glamorous call girl. The popular press, the moving pictures, and television programs all present this glamorous never-ending chase as *LIFE*, with all capitals.

In all this, the object is seldom matrimony; it is rather a way of proving that one is a virile man, or, if one is a woman, then a femme fatale whom men desire. In this day, as most people have become aware through their reading, *love*, all the way from frenzied passion to professional *TLC* (tender loving care), is the goal of all relationships, this at a time when *love* is more often a commodity than an experience. It can be bought for a price and sold to the highest bidder, it seems, instead of freely given as God intended and as Jesus demanded. An illustration of this was the remark of the mother of an unwed pregnant young woman. This mother had only recently found out where her daughter was and why she had ceased to write home. She was horror-stricken that her daughter could have behaved in such a manner considering the careful upbringing she had given her girls. She concluded her outburst with, "How could she sell herself so cheap? I tried to teach both of them not to give away cheaply what they should hold out for marriage." This woman was unaware of the subtle implications of her statement.

The fun morality of our present society has been shown to have an effect both on child raising and on sex standards.[1] "How can anything that is such *fun* be wrong?" is the current question, and sex is touted as the greatest fun of all. But it stops being fun when it changes the shape of the happy players of the game.

All this is to say that instead of a double standard today we have a two-faced look. Illicit coition is one thing, but out-of-wedlock pregnancy is another. In other words, we have not accepted completely what we ourselves are doing. Our clothing, our advertising, our humor, our entertainment, our permissiveness to our young people are all saying romance and glamour are the roadway to "really living," to riches which in turn provide more romance and glamour,

---

[1] "The emergence of fun morality in child rearing, particularly during the 1940's, has been described in considerable detail by Martha Wolfenstein," says Clark E. Vincent in his book, *Unmarried Mothers* (New York: The Free Press of Glencoe, Inc. 1961), p. 8.

as well as freer sex opportunities. The secret hope is that somewhere along this slippery path one will stumble upon love, a love that will prove the pursuit worthwhile and bring satisfaction and privileges won without responsibilities. When it doesn't work this way, when the result is not so favorable as this, and when it becomes physically obvious that sex, not love, has been the bartered commodity, then society, middle-class United States society, cries out in its pain. It is pained today and does suffer with the hurt of its pregnant unmarried population. Society feels the pangs of its own guilt even as it denies its responsibility and involvement. It punishes not itself, but a scapegoat, the young woman who makes it obvious to the society that chastity is not the common ideal. This is not to say that society alone is responsible for the rise in out-of-wedlock pregnancy. Society does, however, provide the climate and the opportunity for the woman to find herself in such a situation.

Clark E. Vincent[2] makes the wise observation that the recent large demand for babies for adoption by middle-class childless families has influenced to some extent the attitudes toward the unwed mother. There is probably more tolerance toward those who make possible good come from an otherwise bad situation than toward those who cause a bad situation to become worse. In other words, as long as white, middle-class babies are available for adoption by white, middle-class families who want them, the mothers of these babies will be regarded with more compassion than the mothers of the nonwhite babies who, some feel, are adding to the population of the already economically distressed, deprived people that are dependent on the taxpaying public for support and livelihood.

The Christian community. While the more secular group of our community are concerned about the serious problem of the unwed mother because of the attendant social problems that arise, the Christian community is more upset because it recognizes its failure as a church to teach its young people the cardinal virtue of chastity. The Ten Commandments and the ethical teachings of Jesus, not to mention St. Paul, are all flouted by every appearance of out-of-wedlock pregnancy. If the sacred precepts of the church and the living

---

[2] Vincent, *op. cit.*, p. 22.

example of truly devout people who make up the church can be disregarded without fear of divine judgment and heavenly wrath, then what is a person to believe? Church leaders are placed in the awkward position of reevaluating virtues in a world that appears to reward what was once called sin. In most cases, sincere efforts are made to accept the young unmarried mother into the church community. Many church people try to accept her in love while at the same time trying not to appear to be condoning her behavior. This is not easy. Generations have quibbled over whether a *bad* deed can be done by a *good* person.

Unwed mothers have claimed over and over again that the thing they most dreaded was to return to their home church in the small town where everybody who didn't know, suspected, and where gossip was the way of life. How much is projection and how much reality one can't say, but it is a stumbling block even among well-meaning Christian people.

The matter of the "second offense" is of special concern in the Christian community, and girls and women who are pregnant out of wedlock repeatedly become a problem in the community as well. This, we believe, does not happen out of sheer cussedness, moral depravity resulting from inherent sinfulness, or overactive sex glands. A person who behaves in such a way is socially, mentally, and emotionally sick, or whatever term your discipline uses to describe the person who cannot live either with himself or with and in society without getting hurt and hurting others. The church more often sees the unwed woman pregnant for the second time than it does the one who is having her fifth child out of wedlock.

We come now to the more specific case of a young woman in the Christian community in which you live. What is the reaction of the people who helped Hallie when she returned from the long visit to her aunt in California? They knew and she knew that they knew that she had had a baby in a maternity home out there. Yet, no one talked openly about it. Now she is beginning to look pregnant again. If you asked ten people what they think about this, probably eight or nine will say something like this: "Well, you can understand one mistake, but after all she went through, if she didn't learn her lesson then, well, I'm not sure we ought to be so lenient." It is difficult to forgive a girl her second out-of-wedlock pregnancy, because few people realize the forces that compel the girl to go through the agony of it all again. Some parents who intend only to be helpful and protective, who believe that pain is best avoided by not mentioning anything connected with it or its cause, ignore the still smoldering ashes of their daughter's experience. Instead of letting the ashes burn out gradually on the open hearth of home, they put a flammable lid of silence on them. The good opportunity such a family has of bringing about a better mutual understanding of each other and of each other's needs disappears. There can be little spontaneity among people worrying lest one of them make a "break." Hence, less and less communication takes place, and the daughter meets once more her former frustrations and tensions, and once more she may try to resolve them as she did before. Then church people become disappointed and often feel as though they, like the parents, have been let down.

Here the pastor and his parishioners can learn from the social worker, who believes that a repetition of behavior that brings unpleasant consequences instead of a satisfactory solution to a person's problem indicates that the further efforts of the agency are needed and will be made available. A review of the person's difficulties may indicate that his life and circumstances must be changed. There is need for more patience and less skepticism on the part of all who work with the "repeater."

The author has talked with many people who hold different points of view concerning the proper role for the counselor of unwed mothers. A more secularly-oriented psychiatric pastoral counselor may seek to help the young woman express herself more fully and adequately, without feeling guilty if she finds sex life more necessary than marriage. A minister may take the first hour of his counselee's time to make her aware of her sin. Another pastor may simply call the maternity home and say, "I've got another one for you." Still another may concentrate on ritual formalities to avoid dealing with human emotions. Of course, there is also the counselor that says to himself, "No, not another," and then takes a deep breath and readies himself to listen to the woman. He is prepared to understand and accept her and suffer with those involved with her because he knows and loves them all. Such varied procedures give one clues to the respective pastoral counselors' attitudes toward sex, sin and forgive-ness. How important to him is the girl who seeks his help? What does he conceive his role to be in such a situation?

The attitude of the unwed mother herself is one of the most in-teresting phenomena to be explored. Before her pregnancy, she usu-ally shares the views of the rest of the young people in the com-munity, because she is not an unwed mother nor does she expect to be. She will avow this most sincerely. If at the time she is having sexual relations with her own particular boy friend she sees this as a private affair, either the privilege of their engaged status or if too young to be engaged, then of their engaged-to-be-engaged status. If something were to happen and she were to become pregnant, then, of course (she thinks) she would marry her boy friend sooner than both of them had planned. It appears as simple as that. Maybe, she half wishes that she does become pregnant, for then her parents would be forced to consent to her marriage as had the parents of some of her friends. These are some of the thoughts spoken by young girls who are members of fellowship groups in churches. The words are echoed by the younger girls in maternity homes. Unfortunately, some girls who become pregnant find that their fiancés show little of their former enthusiasm for early marriage. Indeed, a man may feel that he is being trapped into marriage in such circumstances and begin to see his loved one in a new light. It may be suggested to him that if his girl friend will go all the way with him then maybe she will do the same with lots of others. When he begins to ask himself how she knows that it is his child she is carrying, the idyllic romance is over, and shame and remorse arise.

When a girl first sees the maternity home, she usually says, "Look, Mother, there aren't any bars on the windows!" Inside, she is sur-prised to find girls who could be her neighbors and school mates, not at all the "class" of girls with whom she expected to spend the last weeks of her out-of-wedlock pregnancy.

There is usually a girl in the maternity home who believes she is there because "Everything happens to me." She says, "Of course I don't think being pregnant out of wedlock is all right. But why me? Everyone else has all the fun they want to, and no one else gets preg-nant. Always me. . . . And were my sorority sisters nasty when they found out!" Coition, yes; pregnancy, no.

One 22-year-old girl related her experience in the following way: "I certainly didn't ever intend to let it go so far. It was after the drive-in. We stopped for some French fries and then drove over to the shore—you know—where all the kids park. Well, I was sitting with my feet up—you know—to be more comfortable, and he pulled me closer. I didn't think anything of it. We listened to the music and talked and can you imagine it, it was already one-thirty. I said, 'Oh, my mother will kill me.' 'O.K.,' he said, 'just one more kiss. . . .' Well, here I am. I don't know how I get into such messes but I always seem to do the wrong thing." The girl's attitude was more conservative than her behavior indicated. Her parents who also held similar conservative views regarding sex and moral standards, were greatly distressed when their daughter first showed signs of conspicuous behavior. In fact, they told her, more than once, that they feared the worst. They wondered aloud, within her hearing, whether or not they should have adopted her, inasmuch as they had known the girl's parents were "very common," whereas they considered their own background as an intellectual and artistic one. The girl had great compassion for the unwed mothers she knew, although she considered the state of unwed motherhood as a tragedy to be avoided if humanly possible. Her reasons were that it was not fair to the baby; it was not fair to one's parents whether you could get along with them or not; and it was a terrible thing for a girl to go through.

What are the attitudes of the older unwed mothers? Do they give up whatever morals they have? As society usually says of them, "You'd think they were old enough to know better." Elizabeth, an older girl, had been married and divorced. She found it difficult to live alone with her children without a man. When she refused to have intercourse with her occasional dates, they asked her, "What's the harm? It isn't as though you were a virgin, you know." She has never given up her standards; she did not intend to get pregnant; she is very much ashamed to be pregnant out of wedlock at her age and vows never to yield again no matter how lonely she is.

Flora, a middle-aged woman approaching menopause lived alone without liking it. She found that being a professional woman, and the dependable member of the family, who gave up her life to take care of aging parents, didn't mean that she was able to achieve a satisfying home life of her own. She felt unfulfilled as a woman. Society asks little about the love life or sex life of this kind of woman until she becomes pregnant. Then she is judged more severely than her younger sisters. Her problem probably was more of a psychological nature than that of a widow or even a divorcée with children. She avoided men as a young girl and discovered too late that marriage and a home would have given her more satisfaction than being independent and alone. When this discovery came, it was more difficult for her to be as rigidly moral as she had been when there was less conflict in her life. When her baby was born, her plight was most heartbreaking. She felt it was her last chance, and she asked, "What kind of a mother could I be, beginning at 40 years old, and with no father for my baby?" Marriage was out of the question because the father of the baby is already married. This unwed mother carried a heavy burden of bitterness toward the wife of her child's father for he had convincingly described his wife as a cold, mean, unappreciative woman who refused to grant him a divorce.

When all the people involved in a similar kind of situation are members of his church, the pastor is in for a rough time. The church fellowship is not always at its best when such scandal erupts. People take sides in a predictable pattern, and the pastor must work on many fronts, all because people *react to* rather than help the unwed mother.

Such are the contemporary attitudes held about out-of-wedlock pregnancy and unwed motherhood by our society, by the Christian community, by the clergy, and by the unwed mother herself, both before and after her pregnancy. Many of these are familiar to the reader. Others will become so as he does more work with the unwed mother and her family and, hopefully, with the father of her baby. For the pastoral counselor, however, his own attitude is the crucial one.

Part II

THE BACKGROUND AND DYNAMICS

OF THE UNWED MOTHER

CHAPTER THREE

HER SOCIAL ENVIRONMENT

The question is asked almost every time one hears of an out-of-wedlock pregnancy, "Now why would she do a thing like that? You can't tell me she doesn't know better. She has been brought up to know the difference between right and wrong. She comes from a good family. They're good church people." The most frequent answers are: "Young people go steady much too soon today. They are given too much freedom. They shouldn't drive cars so young. If she had lived at home instead of in an apartment of her own, it never would have happened. What can you expect with all the sexy movies and books and things? They talk about sex so freely in the schools and even in the church today, it gives young people ideas. They should have gotten married."

None of these is the answer to why Jane had a baby out of wedlock; yet none of these can be entirely ruled out as a contributing factor, especially in discussing the young middle-class white girl whose illegitimate baby will shortly be available for adoption. But the unmarried mother has her child out of wedlock for several reasons that can be pointed out without too much difficulty but reasons which are not so easily amenable to correction. First, we must examine the girl's environment, and then the psychological motivations of her behavior. It is wrong to say, although some authorities do, that our culture is entirely responsible for the great increase in the rate of illegal childbearing. It is equally wrong to say, as other authorities do, that a girl becomes an out-of-wedlock mother because she is not able to resolve her personality development problems successfully. And it is wrong to say—as yet no authorities have stepped forward to voice this opinion—that it is because the church has failed in its duty to instill moral standards in its young people. Yet, many pastors feel guilty about this.

Let us say, therefore, that there are a variety of situations in which a young woman of childbearing age may become pregnant if she is predisposed to handle conflicts in this way. This is not to say that such a course of action is usually consciously planned. It is rather to say that such a course is unconsciously acted out in response to given situations that had been a long time in the making. Of course, there are exceptions to this. For example, a woman may live unmarried with her mate over a period of time. The arrangement seems a satisfactory way of life to them. One day they fail to take preventative measures, and she becomes pregnant. In such a case, however, we cannot rule out the possibility of a purposeful accident brought about in an effort to make the living arrangements more permanent.

Another less obvious example, but one which is as much a problem, is that of an engaged girl very much in love. Her wedding date is all set and her gown is chosen. Then she succumbs to the argument that waiting until a certain hour of a certain day to consummate their love is a relic of benighted times. Such persuasion usually results in a quick marriage, less formal than planned, and many recriminations from parents. While such a union is not counted in statistics that we are discussing, it is nevertheless, part of the total problem and one that the pastor is faced with more often than any other.

There is another group of unwed mothers we must consider, those who are not pregnant by choice, and we may thank God that this is a small group. These women become pregnant through assault or rape. While many girls in the first stage of their pregnancy cry "Rape," skillful counseling helps them to become better able to face reality and stop denying their part in the sex act. One must neither assume that the cry of "Rape" is proof of rape nor, on the contrary, that rape is not a possibility.

Some girls have become pregnant through incest, usually as unwilling partners in the beginning when they are not old enough to realize the harm being done to them by their male relatives. When they are old enough to become aware of the tabus, they are usually too involved (sometimes through fear) to protest effectively. Their pregnancy may be a way of getting outside help.

In general, we can say that unmarried girls become pregnant for the following reasons:

1. In the acceptance of premarital coition, they are not cautious;
2. Moral uncertainty and confusion of values are no match for the sexual drives or erotic curiosity;
3. A delinquent pattern chooses out-of-wedlock pregnancy as its symbol;
4. A neurotic need to bear a child out of wedlock and to take it back home to the parents as an effort on the part of the girl to identify with the mother in bearing a child;
5. In a certain strata of society, the stigma attached to out-of-wedlock pregnancy is not nearly so great (in fact may be nonexistent) as the stigma of having no child at all when one is of childbearing age.

As already mentioned, these reasons are based on both environmental and psychological factors. The rest of this chapter will further develop the environmental causes.

Earlier in the book, the plight of the unwed mother in the large city back in the days of more obvious double standards was mentioned. Women came to the city to work in the factories or in large domestic establishments. Her innocence was assumed until she was "betrayed" by almost any man who was so inclined. Then she took to the primrose path that led to the red-light district and a life that was not satisfying nor healthy. These girls were thought of as "bad," or "fallen." These names are still used by polite, middle-class society, which is the standard bearer of our nation, when it speaks of unwed mothers who do not fall into the "it could be your daughter" category. Vincent[1] points out that the "bad causes bad" assumptions of earlier days foster the idea that out-of-wedlock pregnancies are the results of poverty, mental deficiency, broken homes, and so forth, while they obscure the fact that many of the so-called desirable aspects of our social panorama are just as responsible for the problem. He suggests it is more comfortable for us to use the "bad" as a

[1] Vincent, op. cit., pp. 6–12.

whipping boy rather than to expose the "good"—especially the "fun" —as a contributing factor.

While these facts are important in that we become aware of our patterns of thoughts, they are also important because they provide us with more knowledge of the society in which we live and which must be held partly responsible for the problem it claims it wants to solve. People do not look at the relationship between their present standards of morality and the present rate of unwed pregnancy. They do not realize that their attitude implies: "Coition yes, if you can enjoy it and live with yourself; but pregnancy no, or you can't live with us." People are not as alarmed at the increase in adoptable babies or the loose-living arrangements of the student and professional young people as they are about the number of young women served by maternity homes and welfare agencies. What goes on at office parties when the boss is "in his cups" and the girls are being friendly is accepted as a legitimate means of having fun and overcoming the boredom of the routine of the machine age. Each may have reservations about such behavior, but they are smothered by many layers of rationalizations about fun, rights, freedom, nature, popularity, getting ahead, and the like.

There are more arguments against chastity today than there are for it, as every youth counselor knows. Privately and publicly, college students and officials are asking themselves and each other questions about sexual morality. When questions such as, "Whose business is the morality of college students?" are asked in popular magazines, the public is shocked. But the fact that the questions are asked is reassuring to some of the girls. Reading such accounts, they feel that they and their friends are not the only ones enjoying life in a way still frowned on by their parents, yet condoned by implication in the freedom they have to indulge in sexual play with no restraints.

Parents say that they trust their college daughters and sons to behave as they have been taught at home. This is part of the problem. A look into the homes of many respectable church people today presents an example for indulgence, loose-living, and absence of self-discipline that appalls even the liberal-minded counselor. Young people are taught less by precept than by example. It is heartbreaking to watch other girls fight the battle of premarital chastity as long as they can and then know that they surrender, simply because they are no longer asked for dates either alone or in groups. They are sometimes no longer even part of the girls' groups. In a society that prizes popularity more than virtue, there is little satisfaction in being a lonely virgin.

The counselor from one of the churches in a large eastern city voiced his concern for a young working woman whose preoccupation with sex had developed into an obsession. From the suburbs, she moved into a hotel for women but found that she was unhappy there because she could not become part of the group unless she could join in their sex talk, describing experiences in great detail. She bore her isolation as long as she could and finally broke her way into the inner circle by announcing that their talk bored her because they were so inexperienced. She couldn't talk at that level, she said, after having had relations with her own father since her teens. She accomplished her purpose of being accepted into the group, but relied on an element of fantasy that became so powerful that she no longer recognized reality. That was when she decided to speak to the counselor. To be sure, she remained a virgin but at what cost? This story is similar to the ones told to the pastoral counselors in college communities. It takes more strength than most girls possess for them to withstand the pressure of their peers.

What is this obsession with sex? In some cases, it is psychological; in some, a means to an end—status and popularity; and all too often it is a way of experiencing "kicks." For a girl, it is not only the thrill of having intercourse with the man of her choice, the thrill of the physical sensation, but also the thrill of anticipation—something exciting to look forward to or hope for.

We cannot leave this discussion of the morals of our young women and the danger of out-of-wedlock pregnancy, which is always more imminent than young people wishfully think, without claiming that when pregnancy does occur, it may or may not be an accident. When the pressures of succeeding in school, being a credit to one's family, and of deciding what the next move into the future must be are added to the awful struggle for acceptance by one's peers, any girl whose emotional structure is not stable (or who has not been able to resolve problems from the early stages of her development) may

unconsciously wish to become pregnant as a solution to her conflicts.

Briefly having talked about the average middle-class young
woman, for whom the percentage of total out-of-wedlock pregnancies
is less, we must turn to the area of our society where the larger proportion of illegitimacy is to be found, that is, the lower socioeconomic stratum of society. It has been said that no stigma is attached to illegitimacy among low-income groups. However, as
Hyman Rodman said,[2] "Legal marriage and a nonlegal union . . .
are two types of acceptable marital patterns. . . . This is not to say
that these two patterns are equally valued." This statement should
be well noted.

Middle-class norms are often a luxury that the extremely poor
cannot afford even though they might choose to do so. Elizabeth
Herzog,[3] referring to the culture of poverty, calls attention to "the
grinding elements of physical insecurity and deprivation which are
so often neglected" in making generalized statements. She points out
that the poor, deserving or undeserving, are more at the mercy of
circumstances they cannot control than are the rich. This fact influences the perspectives of these people so that they live for the day,
not the future.

These were the conditions of living that were met by Sarah J.
Short,[4] a group worker in a residential area of high social need. In
her address to the Association, she said, "The 'hard to reach unmarried mothers' often come from environments where they have not
had the opportunities to group up and test out what they can do as
individuals. Their subculture defines the primary role of women as
that of having children. All other roles are secondary. This does
not mean that they have been taught to be good wives and mothers."

---

[2] "On Understanding Lower Class Behavior," *Social and Economic Studies,*
Vol. 8 (1959), pp. 441–450.
[3] Elizabeth Herzog, "Unmarried Mothers: Some Questions to be Answered
and Some Answers to be Questioned," *Child Welfare,* (October, 1962), p. 348.
[4] Miss Short, formerly Group Worker at League Park Center in Cleveland,
Ohio, "Effective Techniques of 'Hard to Reach' Out of Wedlock Families,"
May 1963, speech delivered at the Annual Meeting of the Florence Crittenton
League of America.

Miss Short gave the following as characteristics of the Cleveland group of young women with whom she worked:

1. They were unable to see the difference between cause and effect; for example, they failed to see the connection between the sex act and childbirth.
2. Almost all were on Aid-to-Dependent-Children programs.
3. Not legally married, most of them began to have their children at the ages of fourteen and fifteen.
4. A common characteristic was their passive dependency, expressed by them in the remark, "There is always someone who will do it."
5. All the women were present-oriented to the exclusion of the past and future.
6. Contacts with the agencies were at the point of crises; for example, the women appeared at the hospital emergency wards to have their babies.
7. Their lack of controls was reflected in their acting out sexually, etc.
8. Almost all of their children were young and closely spaced.
9. To have children out of wedlock was an accepted part of their culture and did not require institutionalization of any kind.
10. These women were unable to face reality in terms of the standards of the larger society and particularly in terms of authority; for example, "If I cheat, it is my business, and no one will find out anyway."

These characteristics also describe a large segment of the unmarried mothers who are seen by the city hospital chaplain rather than by the pastoral counselor. The reader especially interested in this group should take note of the study of the Aid-to-Dependent-Children program in Cook County, Illinois, in 1960.[5] Even though the major part of the minister's work will not be with the unwed mother in this group, he must be aware of her existence in the community whether he is able to minister to her directly or not.

Consider that the largest number of nonwhite family incomes are between $1000 and $2000 yearly in contrast to white family incomes between $5000 and $6000 yearly. If we use the $1500 yearly income

---

[5] Greenleigh Associates, Inc., 437 Fifth Avenue, New York, N.Y., "Facts, Fallacies and Future: A Study in ADC Program, Cook County, Illinois," (1960).

as the point of referral, 24 percent of the nonwhite and seven percent of the white family incomes fall below it—over three to one.[6]

In his study on the degree of ego involvement in sexual relations of unwed mothers, Clark Vincent made use of statistical data to reach the following conclusion: on a *group basis,* it was (a) closely associated with their socioeconomic status, and (b) associated more closely with their socioeconomic status than with their race.[7]

The study was further corroborated by Chaplain Victor Scalise in his report on sixteen unwed mothers in a state institution, where many of the patients were in the custody of the Youth Service Board or were sent there from a girls' correctional institution. Some of his conclusions were that race seemed less important than environment and that lack of education, few employment opportunities, and inadequate housing were vital factors influencing the lives of these girls. Most of them had committed major or minor infractions of the law, or if they had not violated the law, some member of the family had. The Chaplain was also convinced that all of the patients' relationships had degenerated in part because of these associations and that a high degree of promiscuity was the result. Religious thought played a minor role in their lives.[8]

A Christian minister could hardly say, having read thus far, "Since no unwed mother has come to me for counseling, I do not need to concern myself with the problem. Obviously those in my church are armed against such evils." Unless his parishioners are living in isolation from the world around them, they are all affected by the society in which they exist, no matter how strong their own Christian moral armaments are. If they are to be good neighbors, they must know what their neighbors' needs are. The counselor may not be called upon to help one of his own parishioners, but he should prepare both himself and his people to take their part as responsible citizens in dealing with the problems of the larger community.

Moreover, in many of the maternity homes that we have described,

---

[6] See Herzog, *op. cit.,* p. 346.

[7] Vincent, *op. cit.,* pp. 82–86.

[8] "A Directed Study Report of the Unwed Mother at Tewksbury State Hospital," (April, 1963), Andover Newton Theological School, Newton Center, Massachusetts.

there are a large number of girls of the major Protestant denomina-
tions. Some of these girls had attended Sunday school regularly, had
been confirmed, were leaders of youth groups, had been to conference camps, sang in choirs, and even taught Sunday school. These
are girls whose Christian orientation is unquestionable. While it
cannot be said that there are any known religious causes for out-of-
wedlock pregnancy, neither can it be said that a good Christian
orientation or a thorough knowledge of the teachings of the Christian
church will in itself prevent a tragic situation from happening. Sad,
but true.

CHAPTER FOUR

PSYCHOLOGICAL FACTORS

Out-of-wedlock pregnancy is a serious problem in this country today; not only are a great number of families personally involved and a number of professional people giving help to these families, but it is serious in that the problem has a destructive effect on the personality of a great number of young women, the unwed mothers. Most of these young women, no matter how *unconsciously* they are driven to have out-of-wedlock babies, would not *consciously* choose this way of solving their emotional conflicts. There is no area in this country, no town or city, no economic group or social level, no religious denomination, perhaps no classification of people in our society that does not have to cope with this problem.

We have examined statistics, attitudes of various groups, and the cultural, social, economic, and family environment out of which this problem arises. It increases in complexity as we obtain more information about it, but we must not regard it as hopeless. It may indeed appear so to the person who believes man himself to be the answer as well as the cause of all his problems. But the parish minister or pastoral counselor has a resource beyond himself and his fraternal experts. He wishes to use the growing body of knowledge developed by physical and social science to help his fellowmen understand each other and the world in which they live. He accepts the psychologist's relatively recent discovery that it is in the area of human relationships that man's greatest strides can be made. The religious man accepts this view, because it is as old as religion itself. He remembers the golden rule as an ethic to which almost all civilized nations today subscribe. The Judeo-Christian tradition goes further by stating that we do this as evidence that we love our neighbor as ourself because we love God first with everything we are and have and do.

47

The psychiatrist also is concerned with this loving of neighbor and love of self in mutual exchange. He knows that this is the relationship without which man falls ill. The religious man loves both himself and his neighbor as a child of the God he worships. It is this third dimension of love that is his special resource.

It is no new idea that it is the presence or absence of love in our lives from the beginning that makes the real difference in the quality of our lives. But it may be a new idea to suggest that it is especially the presence or absence of *Agape* in the childhood of girls that influences the *Eros* of their maturity. It is important to see how little girls first experience love, from whom and how they seek it, how they react to its presence or absence in their lives as they progress from infancy through childhood and into adolescence; and as a result of experience and reaction, how they interpret, receive and express love themselves as emerging adults. One can observe how the fantasies of a love-starved little girl may be later acted out so that she becomes an unwed mother. If we have some idea of what has taken place, what is taking place, and what still needs to take place in a young woman's life, our chances of helping her to lead a fuller, richer life are much greater. Since it is in the realm of love where her greatest confusion lies, it is through love that she must be helped. The pastoral counselor is not ready to believe, as the determinist does, that any chain of events or circumstances (including family associations) must overcome the realities of eternal life in the midst of temporal existence. Recognizing and taking into consideration all the evidence revealed in the counseling situation and accepting the fact that some situations do not warrant a good prognosis, nevertheless, our faith holds that God through Christ redeems in his own way and time.

We have looked at the unwed mother as a social creature and have found that she is not very different from her married sisters who are pregnant. But we must now see her as an individual, who is pregnant out of wedlock not just because she subscribes to a new freedom in the moral order, not just because she comes from a stratum of society where women bear children early and late, in or out of wedlock, because illegitimacy is not so much a stigma as legitimacy is a status symbol, and not just because her home conditions have reached a point of intolerability. We must now see her also as a person whose inner conflicts and confusions have become a force to be dealt with and this out-of-wedlock pregnancy is a way of dealing with or, hopefully, resolving them. It is, of course, a self-defeating way. Usually both environmental factors and psychological factors work together to drive the girl into her predicament.

In this chapter on the psychological background of unwed motherhood, we can see how a girl develops from childhood and what can happen during her early years to predispose her to a later out-of-wedlock pregnancy. It is impossible in this context to overstress the primacy of her early experience. Before we look at the developmental stages of childhood, it will help to hold clearly in mind that everything that is said here relates a child to the whole family into which it is born. If we are to understand what has taken place in the homes of many unwed mothers, we must first recognize which of the traditional patterns we cling to in our own lives give meaning to life itself and which are inappropriate and of no intrinsic value. The confusion of poorly defined roles, functions, and relationships gives rise to the problems of the young women we see and seek to help. We look to see what adjustments must be made by both fathers and mothers as well as their sons and daughters.

In today's small or "nuclear"* families there is great emotional concentration. Tensions often build up in the course of a day's work and are not relieved on the job, because good fellowship is supposed to abound. Similarly, there are tensions in the everyday life of a suburban housewife. Although she is provided with labor-saving gadgets, she is expected and expects herself to perform efficiently a dozen jobs at home and in her community. As a result, tensions explode to the chagrin of each parent, and even more dangerously so to the children who often do not know which way to turn for comfort. Small-family conflicts easily become magnified beyond all proportion. The result is a pervading atmosphere of anxiety and tension for which each member feels both a responsibility and guilt. Such a situation occurs especially when a family has compulsively high standards and great expectations for each of its

---

* A family in which there is only the parents and children in contrast to the "family" which includes grandparents, relatives, and household servants.

members. Frequently it is the need to excel and achieve status that has determined that the family shall be a small one. The parents' attention can be concentrated more closely on each other and on the child or children, and their individual performance checked constantly. As a result, there is constant pressure and strain from which emerges protective mechanisms that distort personality. Such a home is frequently the family background of the unwed mother who goes to the maternity home.*

There are many theories about how individuals develop to become the persons they are and each theory divides the growing period into stages. The scheme used here is six stages, which are briefly:

1. Infancy—from birth to two years—the period of maternal nurture, when the baby is helplessly dependent on mother.
2. From two to four years—the period of individuation or growing awareness of the difference between self and non-self.
3. From four to six years—the period when the child begins to differentiate the sexes and to identify herself with her mother.
4. From six to eleven, the period of socialization in a world whose confines are larger than that of her family, a period when previous learning is tested in a new context.
5. From eleven to maturity—the period of struggle to adapt to society as maturity requires and one in which sexual awareness increases.
6. Maturity—the period following adolescence, by which time personal and social integration should have successfully taken place within, and the woman has become a creative individual.

Infancy

1. *The first stage, infancy,* is the period of nurture for the baby girl. Sleeping and eating are the whole of her life, for she sleeps until it is time to be fed. Then she awakens. Should food not be immediately available she begins to howl. While all babies begin to differ from each other as soon as they are born, in one thing they remain alike for some time—when they are hungry they cry for

---

* The counselor will be well repaid for any time he spends reading in the field of family relations.

food. It is not until their experience has been favorable or unfavorable that this pattern changes. If the infant does not receive from her mother the nurture necessary for her sense of well-being, she begins to suffer mistrust. It is here that the basic feeling of *trust or mistrust* in regard to all life begins, and this feeling can become an underlying attitude toward everything and everybody as time goes on. A mother's way of nurturing her little one cannot be explained to the baby; it must be experienced to be understood. If the mother has no idea what nurture means beyond a bottle every four hours, her child will not know either, but she will feel that she is living in a world that cares nothing for her. She may experience this as a lack within herself, which will grow into a feeling of inferiority. In this case, the girl will grow up with the lowest possible opinion of herself. At this point, the needs of the baby, not the mother, determine the success of bringing a baby through the first year of life.

Not only is a pattern of trust or mistrust established during this period, but also the pattern of handling angry impulses. Anyone who has ever observed a baby who is nearly convulsed with rage because she is not being fed as soon as she thinks she should be has seen a primitive display of anger. What cannot be seen is the accompanying fantasy of swallowing up the whole world. If mother and child are enjoying their experience of nurture, and the little one trusts her mother, sooner or later these angry rages will taper off and nobody will be the worse for them. Mother understands them and accepts them as part of baby's growing pains and baby feels free to express her displeasure without fear of retaliation.

This is the beginning of impulse control. Where there is complete trust, the mother can set limits, which are an expression of love for her child. Then the child can even bear the frustration of finding herself impotent (as an infant) instead of omnipotent. Thus she not only learns to control her impulses, but also gets satisfaction from doing it. Unfortunately, many parents never learned through their own experience that limit-setting is a loving and necessary part of a child's wholesome development. If they felt limits were imposed on them in anger, they will hesitate to set limits for their own children—except in anger. So once again the children's teeth are set on edge, because the parents ate sour grapes.

If the mother regards her baby's rage as unacceptable behavior, the baby may hide it—literally, swallow it—to avoid her displeasure. Under such circumstances, she cannot outgrow her infantile anger. As she grows older, she fears the anger she tries to hide because of its destructive nature and because of the retaliation and punishment it may evoke toward herself. Therefore, she represses it, that is, convinces herself it is not there. When it is repressed it becomes generalized, which means that there is an angry undercurrent in all relationships, of which the girl is not aware.

Soon the baby becomes aware of more than food. She feels as though she and her mother are one. This is called *primary identification*. Mother is there to supply her need for food, warmth, and softness. The sound of Mother's voice, which baby soon recognizes, is important to her. In fact, Mother's very presence is gratifying. It is a time when the baby appears to think she owns the world and that it is run for her sole benefit. It is appropriate for a baby to feel that she controls the world about her at this age (which in truth she seems to do), but if fantasies of omnipotence continue as she grows older, it is an indication of an emotional disturbance that has its origin in this period. If the little one has been ignored and has felt helplessly uncared for, her only satisfaction will be derived from these fantasies of controlling the world. A beautiful nursery and a silver spoon are no substitute for maternal nurture.

Fortunately for all of us, the baby can tolerate a degree of unsatisfactory nurture and frustration before she is harmed by it, else who would survive? However, since reasonableness is not one of baby's assets, the baby cannot understand why her mother must leave her, whether it is for a few hours, weeks, months, or forever. Substitute care is not the same, but can be tolerated for short periods if the child is happy and secure with her mother the rest of the time. Moving the child from one foster home to another produces an effect similar to that caused by the abandonment of the baby by the mother. Since the child is totally dependent on support from outside, and since she feels her mother to be part of herself, she feels helpless, withdraws, and becomes apathetic if there is no mother to depend upon.

Individuation

Discriminating between Self and Non-self

2. *The next stage, from two to four years,* is the period of individuation, or the age of learning to discriminate between the self and non-self. The baby now begins to learn that she and her mother each have a self. It is accomplished without difficulty if there is a loving relationship, if the baby can feel secure that the mother will be there with her when she reaches out for her. Independence and mastery begin to be acquired. The tyranny of the baby lessens as her helplessness lessens. The fantasy of omnipotence remains only if independence and mastery are for some reason not possible at this point. This is the beginning of social behavior—eating by herself, talking, walking, and being toilet trained, as well as exploring the world about her with all her senses. The baby begins to seem more like a little girl. As she submits to parental discipline, she begins to absorb (take into herself, introject) the standards and ideals of the family. What she learns in love, she learns positively, and it becomes useful to her later as her conscience. The behavior that brings mother's love and approval at this stage determines the pattern she will pursue, and the way she will pursue it will become her way of being herself. Then, as she becomes more aware of other members of the family, she incorporates into her self some of their ways as well until they all become a part of her.

If, however, things were not going well between this little one and her mother back in the earlier stage when nurture was most important, she may not be able to come through this stage of individuation as well. If things have gone well up to this point, but trouble arises between the mother and the baby now, the baby will remain dependent and more or less emotionally infantile. The baby needs to feel that her mother loves her as she seeks by trial-and-error to master the baby tasks expected of her. If there is difficulty in the toilet training and the child feels pushed to "give" what she is not yet ready to give up, she will react with a tendency to retain whatever she can. Furthermore, if this stage does not go well, the little girl may become preoccupied with doing everything just so, giving overattention to detail.

Sexual Differentiation

3. *Sexual differentiation, between four and six years,* is the period during which the child begins to recognize that she is a girl and must grow up to be like her mother instead of her father, although at this stage she loves him more than she does her mother, and she wants to have him all to herself. At this time, she must learn that she cannot possess him, but that if she becomes like her mother, she will some day have a husband of her own to love. It is the identification with the parent of one's own sex (boy or girl), which resolves the loss of the other parent as a "love object" that one can possess.

As a result of this process of identification with her mother, the little girl begins to have a picture of herself in her mind. This picture is called the "ego ideal." This process is well described in a Hollywood movie called *The Secret Life of Walter Mitty.* The film tells of a mild, timid man, who has grandiose daydreams in which he plays heroic roles that he certainly would not attempt to perform in his real life. All of us at this age begin to have daydreams or *fantasies* of ourselves as we should like to be and toward which we strive, either realistically or unrealistically. If the little girl has become mistrusting, angry, or has not successfully met the problems she faced in the first two stages of her life because she felt an absence of loving, her fantasies will be of a kind that compensate for her loss. She will then, in fantasy, find love, punish mother, and enjoy the sensations she has missed. The more deprived a child is, the more time she spends in fantasy rather than in the world of reality. Her ego ideal will be the Cinderella of her natural self, endowed with whatever else is necessary to capture Prince Charming (who is really father), to punish the wicked stepmother (her own mother), and triumph over the ugly sisters. The further from reality the ego ideal is, the more frightening it is to look at this difference honestly. She will go to great lengths to avoid being tested or challenged, because if the test came and she could not meet it, she would have nothing to sustain her. For her, the image is reality until it is destroyed. Then, by her own evaluation, she has nothing. In some cases, however, instead of an idealized image, there is such a low self-image or self-esteem that the only role possible to assume is that of perpetual failure or scapegoat. A self-image of this sort arises as the result of severe deprivation at the earliest stage.

It was during the previous stage of development that preparation was made for the little girl's *conscience* to form. Earlier, all the do's and don't's from outside become the *internalized oughts and ought-nots*. If they are learned in an atmosphere of love, if mother and child have happily come through the early stages, then the conscience, which forms now, will be a good, healthy inner guide. The girl will feel guilty for her transgressions, but she will not be overwhelmed by an accompanying shame. She will, instead, be able to meet the normal demands of her conscience for punishment through reparation and forgiveness. In this way, her guilt is resolved.

If, however, an *overdeveloped conscience*[1] is formed at this time, a girl will seldom get in trouble, for she will keep her emotions under tight control. This kind of conscience is formed when, for some reason, the child does not develop emotionally as she should. She sees life through the eyes of a two-year-old rather than from the perspective of a normal four- or five-year-old, and therefore she interprets her mother's actions in the light of her own intense infantile feelings. The resulting internalized picture of authority is that of a cruel slave driver. This girl's need to endure suffering will dominate her behavior. Normal pleasure will arouse feelings of guilt within her. She will become puritanical as she grows older.

An *undeveloped or useless conscience* may be formed as the result of any of the following reasons:

1. If the mother (or other authority figure) is weak or incapable, overpermissive or uninterested in guiding a child, the conscience cannot develop well.

---

[1] We have here drawn on the material of Paul H. Gray, "Conscience, Guilt and the Unwed Mother," Journal of Pastoral Care, Vol. 13, No. 3, (Fall, 1959).

2. If the mother follows the do-as-I-say-not-as-I-do pattern, the child will do the opposite and accept the opposite as her standard.
3. If there has been no primary identification with mother or mothering person, because she was not available either emotionally or physically, no stable image can be used in the conscience formation process.
4. When hatred for mother develops and the girl is unable to identify with her, the conscience may form and be exacting, but it is repressed and becomes useless as a guide. However, the demands for punishment by her repressed conscience are met by the self-destructive nature of her activties. This is the out-and-out rebellious girl.

All of what has been said points out the importance of a little girl's being able to accept her mother as the model upon which can be built an ideal image for herself and from which she can internalize her permissions and prohibitions—her conscience. She also learns that her father belongs to her mother and that some day, she, like her mother, will have a husband whom she will love and by whom she will be loved. If she can learn this, she will know what every mature woman knows, that there is a new kind of satisfaction in the pain of renunciation.

What has just been said seems a long way from a portrait of Judy, the littlest angel in the Christmas pageant as she sits on daddy's knee looking up into his adoring face. Judy's mother and father, like most parents, are not aware what their children are experiencing in response to their best parental efforts. They try to raise their children so that they will be a credit to themselves, to their parents, and to the society around them. It is this very compulsion to perfection and achievement on the part of most middle-class Americans today that obscures the love they really feel for their children. But the children are not mindreaders. The little girl who has not learned to trust during the period of nurture, who has not learned independence and mastery when she was able to stand on her feet and explore her physical environment, and has not been able to accept mother as her model of the woman into which she will grow, this little girl finds obstacles in life that may become insurmountable during adolescence.

Socialization

4. *Socialization, or latency,* comes *between the seventh and eleventh years.* It takes place in the widening world of the girl as she meets new people and has new experiences beyond the confines of her home and family. The school and the community are now an extension of her family. She begins to learn from older people, who become, for her, parent substitutes. Even more important to her, are other children of her own age against whom she measures herself. She weighs the patterns and learning she has already acquired and tests them against social reality. She learns what will happen when she gets "too fresh" or tries to push other little girls around. She learns how to get along with her playmates and schoolmates in the best way she can. The child discovers that other people do not always react the same as members of her family have, so that while her urges are the same as always, she may have to find other ways of satisfying them that are acceptable in her new world.

During this period, there is also an exploration of the sexual role. Sometimes, this results in physical experimentation, which upsets the parents of the children if they view it as they would similar actions among older children. To them, it is an ill omen. Mostly, exploration of the sex role is concerned with what is expected of little girls and how they should do it. For instance, they learn among other things that girls are supposed to keep clean, not be fresh, act like little ladies, and that boys are not supposed to hit girls no matter what girls do to provoke them. While these admonitions are not of tremendous importance in themselves, they do have importance as they contribute to a child's interpretation of his or her own sex role for some time to come. This is not a period of further psycho-sexual development, but it does help to prepare the youngster for the subsequent adolescent struggle. You only have to observe any group of youngsters of this age to recognize those who have come happily to this stage of their development and those who have not. Yet, they are all growing and learning. Fortunately, much of what they are now assimilating will stand them in good stead, because there may be relationships and experiences that serve to counterbalance some of the unpleasant earlier experiences.

At this time, as at any other, if the experiences of meeting the world beyond the door become too unpleasant and demand more of a child than she can give, she may regress, that is, try to return to one of the earlier stages, at which time she felt more secure and more able to cope with her environment in her own way.

Adolescence

5. *Adolescence, from eleven until maturity,* which is usually thought of as beginning at eighteen or nineteen, is the stage of struggle to adapt to society as maturity requires. The sex drives are new and frightening, and they bring with them the awakening of the conscience which began forming during the earlier years of life. The problem of *role* has to be dealt with—not only the role of a man or role of a woman—but the role of a human being. The "Who am I?" and the "What am I?" must be at least partially answered, and yet dealing with verbal abstractions is never more difficult. As pointed out in the second stage of individuation, the child selects what seems to her the desirable aspects of several persons or parts of various roles she has encountered. She must now integrate these into a consistent, harmonious pattern if she is to become a maturely functioning adult.

The struggle that took place back in the four- to six-year-old period must now be worked through again, but this time outside the family. What goes on during this time is a good indication of the stage of development to which a young girl has really progressed—if one can see the girl beneath the trappings of glamour and apparent sophistication.

This is the time when the self must be finally and distinctly emancipated from the parents. Often, the only acceptable proof of this seems to be a full-scale rebellion. A pitched battle, however, should be unnecessary. Emancipation may wear many faces, appear in many places, and does not happen all at once. But happen it must, if wholesome maturity is to be achieved.

As the pastor views this, he may observe that some parents are themselves so confused about what it means to be maturely functioning men or women and so unsure of their own roles in the family that they cannot provide healthy models for their children. Adolescents may come to him for help, because they feel that their parents are more confused than they are. They want to know how they can possibly please their angry parents when their parents treat them as little children, who must obey every command. Yet, they insist that their children assume adult responsibilities. If the parents were perfect, the adolescent would still have some of these feelings. But few parents are perfect, and some of these feelings are justified in reality.

The girl who reaches adolescence without resolving her basic conflicts, and who is not able to make the necessary sexual differentiation during the period of sexual differentiation, may now turn to men for the kind of *maternal love* of which she feels deprived, just as she turned to her father for it in the past. She wants to be held, cuddled, and "loved," and she will accept sexuality as the price she must pay for it (although this is not a thought process). This young girl's need for a love-substitute is a long way from the common concept of her being "free with men because she is oversexed." As she seeks this affection, she puts herself in a position to be misunderstood by her male partners.

This girl unconsciously needs to have a baby herself in order to feel any identification with her mother. In her fantasy, she will be the good mother. In her fantasy, she takes the baby home to her mother, with the hope that Mother will now be the good mother, which she wasn't before. A loss of someone, or something, she loves may be the trigger that causes her to act out this fantasy that she may have had for some time. However, when reality interrupts this dream, and she finds herself pregnant with a baby, which she cannot take home but must give up, her basic problem remains unsolved, and there can easily be a repetition of the acting out of the fantasy, unless the personality disturbances are resolved with the aid of a skilled therapist. It does no good to explain the dynamics of psychology to the unwed mother; she must discover the truth of them in her own life. Fortunately, many times the very crisis her unwed pregnancy creates provides the opportunity for solution, for both she and her parents are led to examine their respective roles and to see how better communication can take place among the *three* of them.

Maturity

6. *Adulthood, or maturity,* is the *final stage* of development. By this time, integration should have occurred, one's style and attitudes have emerged, and one's values and future goals have been established. When maturity arrives, the early pleasure principle of childhood, which is characterized by the need for immediate satisfactions, gives way to the ability to work toward a greater good in the future. With true maturity, also, comes the kind of independence that recognizes and accepts mutual interdependence.

The mature woman, then, is an integrated person, who knows that she is a woman and not a shapely, glamorous childbearing man. She accepts her role as a woman and is not ashamed of that passivity which is an aspect of womanliness. She has values derived from her religious faith that determine her moral and ethical standards. She has the capacity for enjoyment, but her pleasures are not her first concern. As a mature woman, her greatest concern is for those whose care is her responsibility, yet she does not need to possess them to love them, nor does she need proofs and reassurances of their love for her. She can ask for help and can give help without feeling obligated or beholden. In brief, she loves and is loved, because as the great commandment says, "You shall love your neighbor as yourself."

This degree of maturity is rarely to be found in an unmarried mother in our society. The reason is that such maturity is evidence that either the developmental stages were successfully resolved as they were passed through or that they were subsequently worked through in therapy. The unwed mother still has unresolved problems, often basic needs which she is trying unsuccessfully to solve by her present behavior. It can be repeated here that the crisis of unwed motherhood is often the first step toward solution. It can also be said, encouragingly, that maternity is, for many girls, a maturing experience in itself, for it may be accompanied by an altruistic love not previously felt. From these beginnings, there can arise a measure of independence gained through initial efforts at problem-solving with a long, as well as immediate, viewpoint. These exercises are a sort of belated training for maturity.

Summary

We began this chapter about the psychological background of the unwed mother by pointing out that there is undeniably a group of unwed mothers who are pregnant out of wedlock for reasons other than those discussed in Chapters Four or Six. They have become pregnant not by conscious choice in most cases, but because they are unconsciously motivated to do so in an effort to solve some basic underlying problems that interfere with their potential for establishing a creative life. These girls seem to bury their God-given talents, and they settle for second-rate satisfactions. Such behavior is always mystifying to friends and relatives. We recognize the need for help by interpreting the forces that drive these girls along the road to unwed motherhood, while we deny that such a girl's direction is irreversible beforehand, or hopeless afterward. We allow for the work of the Spirit even while we gird ourselves to join the battle if called upon to do so.

As each child comes into the family at a different stage in the life of the family unit, she experiences her parents and her brothers and sisters in a way different from their experiences of each other and of herself. In other words, although it is the same family, the environment and relationships vary, as does the physical heredity. One does not have the same expectations for all the Smith children. We followed the theory of how a child develops from a helpless and omnipotent-feeling baby, from a toddler who discovers she can walk away from mother as well as toward her, to a child who is "in love with" first one parent and then the other and finally discovers which one she "must" follow as a model. During this time, she learns what is right and wrong or, better, what her parents conceive to be right and wrong. Eventually, she discovers that she can determine this for herself at the dictates of her own developing conscience. Then she widens her circle and socializes with not only parent or authority figures, but with her own age or peer group as well. This is an important period of testing herself to find out whether what she has learned is usable. Do her patterned responses work *for* her and is she really like the playmates of her own sex? In the next stage of adolescence, her conscience is reawakened, for it must deal with sex urges, which though they may frighten her also transform her. The rapid changes in her life sometime change her into a prude, an idealist, a rebel, an adult, and a child. By the time chronological and physical maturity is possible, a pattern of either adult, adolescent, childish, or infantile behavior has been established.

If there have been too many impediments to healthy development along the way, emotional conflicts ensue which affect the whole character or personality of the girl and woman. In the case of the unwed mother, childish fantasies remain with her until such time as they are compulsively acted out, and the result is that she becomes pregnant.

The usefulness of the foregoing material will become relevant when the counseling process is examined. The families in the community of the pastoral counselor and parish minister are what they are, for better or worse, but no family in trouble should be without help if it seeks help through the Christian church. The pastor who understands what goes on in the life of any family, and the family of the unwed mother in particular, is better able to help at a time of such need, because he can say to the unwed mother or her parents, "I understand," and mean it. He no longer need say, "Too bad, such a fine family. I can't understand it." He can guide them toward the sources of physical, social, and mental rehabilitation, as well as offer them spiritual help, so that their wholeness may be restored.

We have covered a great deal of ground rapidly up to this point in preparation for what is the real purpose of this volume, which is to be of specific help to the pastor who will counsel the unwed mother.

CHAPTER FIVE

A CASE STUDY—EVA

In the foregoing chapter we have seen how the personality of a girl develops. If all goes well and she goes through each stage satisfactorily, she reaches maturity ready to cope with any of the exigencies common to the average mature person. If, on the other hand, her basic needs during the infancy period are not met satisfactorily, then she is also deprived of other normal experiences in the subsequent stages of her development, because she is not ready for them. Although her emotional development is retarded or, in more serious cases, arrested, she does grow up physically and with the intelligence expected of her so that she seems to be a "normal" girl. This is what makes it so difficult for the lay counselor, parents, and the young people themselves. When everything *seems* to be going along all right, an out-of-wedlock pregnancy comes as a shock to all, for the young mother's behavior cannot be understood by the other members of her family.

The story of Eva typifies this situation very well. You might say, Eva was expected rather than hoped for. Before she was born, her mother worked, and afterward she was eager to return to her job to help support the family. Therefore, Eva was taken from her mother's breast and given a bottle in a holder as she lay in her crib. She missed the warmth and bodily contact of her mother, which the baby sitter felt she was not paid to give. Eva howled, but received no satisfaction, only colicky frustration. She became what is called a cranky baby and was left more alone. She had to be quiet to be picked up. She learned not to express her anger, but her anger did not diminish. A little later, she found that everyone around her was even more impatient and unfriendly when she soiled her diaper. Then very soon, too soon for her understanding, it was even more unacceptable for her to soil her training pants. Her working mother had little time for "unnecessary" laundry and extra cleaning. (Such a mother may work for the church, either as a volunteer or paid worker, or as a nurse or teacher. She is usually an altruistic person and loves children, but her patience is limited.) Eva's mother showed more efficiency than affection.

Eva was becoming a conscientious little girl, never unruly, neat in appearance, and tidy with her toys. She was a model child, so little trouble that her mother could leave her with anyone, if necessary. As she grew a bit older, she turned to her father for the affection her mother hadn't given her. Such a child as Eva would have fantasies at this time that Father would be all hers, that she would take him away from the cruel mother and get even with her. Her father was very loving when he was loving, but he was moody. He obviously resented the fact that Eva's mother was the real worker of the family. He was not considered as dependable as he was charming, and often he was neither. Eva would accept his attentions when they were forthcoming, and efface herself when he was in a "mood." During her adolescence, Eva's mother and father had severe marital difficulties. Eva felt guilty, for she believed that somehow she was the cause of them. In her fantasy, of course, she had caused it, purposely, and that is why she felt guilty. She also had feelings of worthlessness, which led her to believe that she must have displeased her father. While he showed his affection for her much of the time, he often didn't want her around. Then, when both parents used Eva to salvage their marriage, she felt unequal to the burden. She was sure that she was letting them down. She couldn't know that they were completely unaware of her feelings. If only she could make her father love her all the time as he did sometimes, she wouldn't mind not measuring up to her mother's standards. Her fantasies continued. Her mother never showed any anger. She was too well controlled for that. Eva was sure that her mother seldom was angry, and she envied her the peace of mind that she thought that her mother enjoyed despite the serious family difficulties. She was jealous of her capable and efficient ways and tried, without conviction, to compete. She was afraid she might get someone else "down on her" and, increasingly, she couldn't bear such a thought. She supposed, hopefully, that someday she would marry someone like her father, but she knew better than to expect such good fortune.

In the meantime, her family planned that she was to finish school and get a job. She yielded to her mother's wishes and took a commercial course in school, where she excelled at bookkeeping. However, she was terrified that she would not graduate. When she did, both her mother and father were proud parents. She had made them proud. Everyone was proud. Her father gave her an expensive charm bracelet as a graduation present and called her his wonderful, big, grown-up girl. Her mother said she was sure now that Eva would get a fine job and be a real credit to them. Then she reminded her that this was only the beginning. Eva had felt it was an end in itself but now she discovered that she was expected to keep going, going, going. Her mother also said it was a shame that her father spent all that money on such a foolishly extravagant gift especially since he owed so much on his car. Some other things happened that graduation day, too. Eva took her mother's car and drove for hours into the night. She ended her journey at the apartment of a newly married friend. Unfortunately the friend was away and her husband, an old friend of Eva's, was home alone. He and Eva solaced each other. The few who knew where Eva spent the following fall and winter wondered whatever caused Eva to get pregnant out of wedlock. She was such a good girl, not wild like most high schoolers, and she had such a promising future. They didn't know about the life Eva had led for eighteen bad years, how she felt helpless, worthless, and unloved until she discovered her father could give her the satisfactions that her mother never had. Eva felt that her mother was unreasonable and demanding. She was angry, but didn't realize it, because she repressed her anger till she herself was not aware of it. She also was unaware that her love for her father was not a healthy love. This, too, escaped the notice of others.

Everyone was shocked to learn that Eva had a sexual relation with her friend's husband. But here again, when the whole story became known, that act, too, fell into place in the puzzle. Her graduation day was a crisis for her. The joy that she experienced when she received a beautiful gift from her father was nearly destroyed by her mother's reminder that he had done the wrong thing, that his obligations lay elsewhere. Then her pleasure at achieving the status of a graduate was short-lived because her mother told her this was fine, but it was only a beginning. Eva reached the point where nothing could provide her with satisfaction. Her life was emptiest just when she had expected fulfillment. She escaped from this unbearable reality by acting out her earlier fantasy. She would be like her mother, only a better mother. Symbolically, she stole her father (her friend's husband) away from her mother (her absent friend) and filled her (emotional) emptiness with a baby.

The young man, who became the father of her baby, meant no more to Eva than any casual acquaintance. Even her own father had not met her real need, for her father's love had always been only a substitute for her mother's, which Eva still needed.

Eva's out-of-wedlock pregnancy represented her attempt to gratify infantile impulses. The community viewed it as a transgression of the moral and social standards, and her act hurt her parents. Her mother had no idea of what was going on in Eva's mind or how her own earnest actions and sincere remarks were being distorted in the child's mind. She was kept busy in trying to hold the family together by functioning in the roles of both father and mother. There was a confusion of role on the part of all three, but no one in Eva's family was any better or any worse than the average family in any church today. This is what poses the problem for the pastor. Unless some member of such a family seeks pastoral help before the act of disaster, the tensions will probably not be resolved. If a pastor can reach such a parent as Eva's mother and help her to become more keenly aware of her daughter's needs and reactions, better communication might be established between mother and daughter. Thereafter, each can come to know the other better. The damaged human relationship can be restored, and the daughter's compulsion to act out infantile needs will be abated. When parent-child communications break down, it is the parent who must repair the damage. The wise parent will know that communication is more than just a verbal process.

While we have dwelt on the unconscious forces that impel a girl into out-of-wedlock pregnancy, it is important to remember that her conscious drives also create problems and provide impetus for her actions. Whereas the unconscious forces give rise to a girl's predisposition to out-of-wedlock pregnancy, it is the forces of which the girl is conscious, which precipitate it. However, if the predisposition is compelling enough, a girl will plan a strategy to become pregnant, even though her conscience protests. The conscience is seldom any match for a deep-seated emotional drive to seek basic satisfactions that have been denied. Most girls that seek the pastor's help with their out-of-wedlock pregnancy problems are those whose conscience is still active and who feel shame because of their action. Their conscious intention never was to become pregnant out of wedlock. They have, with a few reservations, accepted the moral precepts of the church even while they have questioned them. But, the mere acceptance of a code of morality is not enough to prevent this kind of out-of-wedlock pregnancy.

Part III

THE COUNSELING PROCESS

CHAPTER SIX

The MINISTER As COUNSELOR

Not very long ago two young women from the same city went to the same maternity home within a year of each other. One told the chaplain that she had not confided in her own minister when she learned of her pregnancy. She felt that he would not keep the matter in strict confidence, nor would he be helpful. The second girl said that she had gone immediately to her minister and that he was helpful both to her and to her parents through the first shocking days. Furthermore, the minister continued to be helpful in the pastoral role. The chaplain knew that both girls were describing the minister of Pilgrim Church in Central City.

One girl thought that her minister would judge the family and betray their confidence. The other girl believed in her minister and found him to be an understanding counselor and friend. One may honestly question whether or not this minister, or any other for that matter, could have helped the first family as he helped the second. The minister still works under the handicap of a stereotype, as does the unwed mother. It is not necessarily the fault of the minister that his parishioners do not turn to him for counseling when problems arise from out-of-wedlock pregnancy. More and more frequently, they do, if we take into account the number of referrals made by the clergy to social agencies and the ministers' own statements of their experience.

The minister's own family is not necessarily immune to the upheaval of out-of-wedlock pregnancy. As one unmarried mother said when another criticized the imperfections of the clergy, "They're people like the rest of us; some good, some not so good, some helpful. . . ." Her words drifted off with her shrug. Ministers are people who achieve the same degree of personal and parental perfection and imperfection as the people in their parishes. Out-of-wedlock pregnancy is not unknown to the parsonage or manse. When it does occur there, it is seldom handled with the understanding and flexibility necessary for rehabilitation. Ministers frequently become more frightened when they are personally involved in such a situation than those they counsel. This is not surprising for few clergymen are prepared to admit that such a crisis could befall their home life. Little or no attention has been given to the subject in seminary, graduate studies, religious literature, or pastoral conferences until recently. And, unless one accepts the possibility that such a situation could happen at home, one's help with a neighbor's misfortune will be less sensitive than it is perfunctory, proficient, and lacking in grace.

Another consideration that affects one's ministry to the unwed mother is the theological background of the minister and the cultural pattern of his parish. This can be illustrated by the experience of one pastor, who had never had occasion to talk with an unwed mother. The semirural community of Riverton in which his church was located was homogeneous and adhered closely to the tradition of the elders. There was no other church nearby. The citizens and the church members were the same kind of people. Then, like many beautiful, unspoiled communities of its kind, Riverton was suddenly overwhelmed by a large housing development called River Meadows. What had once been a quiet little village became a dormitory town for a large industry located about five miles away. A church of another persuasion was built almost immediately. The young people of "Old Church," as it was soon called, went to school with the children of the new families. There was a clash of standards. Entertainment and recreation so commonly accepted today, but which had been expressly forbidden by "Old Church" tradition, now appeared both alluring and available—especially since the newcomers had cars for their use. The effort of the old church to keep its sons and daughters apart from the life of the new community failed, and soon some of the more obvious signs of the twentieth century began to appear. The old inhabitants of the town found cosmetics, tobacco, and dancing no farther away than the newly opened canteen; they went in the cars of their new friends to drive-in movies, etc.

Then came the first case of out-of-wedlock pregnancy. It was the girl's family that consulted the pastor. They felt that a sin had been committed by a member of their family, and therefore the matter should be handled by the church. It was heartbreaking for all concerned. There was no question of the girl ever returning to school. The suggestion of marriage was rejected by both of the young people, who had no thought of any permanent relationship. This, in itself, was almost the greatest shock. There was nothing to be done, the pastor felt, but for the girl to repent and ask God's forgiveness, and then to settle down and raise her child. This was done. The church community tried to tighten its control, which served only to increase the problem. Three more high-school girls became pregnant within two years. The minister was crushed. He grew very depressed, considered himself a failure, and wanted to leave his parish and forsake the ministry.

It came to the pastor's attention that there were ways by which the young mother did not have to raise her "love-child" alone. What he had hoped would be an example of the evils of tobacco, dancing, and movies proved to be no deterrent. The pastor then wrote to a maternity home asking for an appointment to present his problems as he saw them and to learn of other resources in addition to the ultimate resource, God. Of course, he was still mainly concerned with the moral defect in the character of the unwed mother and the atonement she must make. Nevertheless, over the next few years, when an unwed mother came to him, he would help the girl and her family by arranging to seek aid for them from social agencies and a physician as well as by guiding them spiritually. It was not necessary for him to alter his religious belief about the sin involved, but he did need to change his concept of what was to be done about it, and what part of this burden the newborn child should bear. His own moral fortress was so impregnable that it was difficult for him to conceive the relatively unfortified code of ethics on which many earnest Christians rely today.

This illustration, which reads as though it were a page torn out of an old book, is presented here because it is a boldly clear picture of an often too subtle parish situation in which the minister is caught and for which he is ill-prepared. Most ministers do not have such a closed and inflexible church group as "Old Church," and newcomers to the town may not upset the equilibrium of his parish to such a great extent. Nevertheless, there are many innovations, as shown in the previous chapters, which do make a difference to the life of the people. Any time this happens, tragedies will occur in the lives of some families, who have built their homes on too rigid or too permissive a basis. While the pastor helps his members to meet constructively the threat, reexamining and strengthening values, he must be ready to help the individuals who fall as casualties, insofar as he can, to reestablish themselves in the community and to regain their spiritual health.

The minister is seldom immune from the dilemmas confronting the layman when he is forced to make an ethical choice. Unfortunately, there is rarely a simple choice between right and wrong, good and bad. The range for selection may be between bad and worse, or it may be between good and better. It may be that there is no "good" solution to one's problems. In his pastoral role the counselor will want to help the unwed mother find the "best" solution applicable to her present and future welfare.

The following are some of the dilemmas that pastors have faced as they worked with unwed mothers and their families:

1. A girl tells you, but not her parents, that she is pregnant. The parents come to you, anxious about her unusual behavior. What do you tell them or what do you do?

2. You know who the father of the baby is, because the unwed mother has told you. He has taken no responsibility for his part in the situation. Subsequently, he becomes engaged to a girl in your parish and plans to marry her. He has told his fiancée nothing of his past relationship and the baby. What do you do?

3. When a girl from a neighboring parish comes to you because she refuses to see her own pastor, do you enter a counseling relationship with her?

4. The unwed girl and her mother, especially her mother, want your "permission" to bring suit against the father of the baby, not because they need the money but "because he must be punished to protect other innocent girls." What is your advice?

5. The young man is a protégé of yours, whom you hope to interest in the ministry. As the result of the affair he has with a Roman Catholic girl from an unfavorable family background,

the girl becomes pregnant. She is interested only in marriage. Can you look at this objectively?

6. You know the unmarried mother is in a maternity home. Her parents do not know of her situation as they are away, and she has not written to them about it. She has exacted your promise not to reveal her whereabouts. An aunt of the girl comes to you and surprises you with: "I've been trying to locate Sarah, and I'm told she is in Florida. I don't believe that, but I am sure that you know where she is. Her landlady said that you called on her before she left. I'm very worried about her as I feel responsibile while her parents are away. Now you know you can trust me; we've been old family friends for years. Please tell me where Sarah is and if there is anything wrong, or anything I can do to help her." What do you say to this aunt? (She doesn't give up easily!)

7. One of the families in your parish wants to adopt a child and has been turned down by several agencies. They know that there is a young woman in the parish, who is pregnant out of wedlock. They come to you with the proposition that they will pay all expenses of the girl if you can persuade her to let them adopt the baby. What would you do?

8. What is your reaction to the "lies" the girls and their families feel that they have to tell to protect themselves and each other socially in your community and parish? What do you tell these people when they ask you if this is right or wrong, if it is a sin or a social maneuver? Do you believe that answering all inquiries or insinuations with "I never talk about my parishioners" protects their confidences? How do you deal with your own conscience?

9. The family physician says that he can perform a therapeutic abortion in a certain case, because he says that having a baby would be injurious to his patient. This is a very wealthy family. They want your opinion of this abortion. What is it? How do you feel about the family that plans to take their daughter to Canada for an abortion at the expense of the alleged father, who has made the arrangements? They want to know if this would be adding to the sin already committed. What would you tell them?

10. Berle wants to bring her baby home and raise it within her family, with no attempt to hide the fact that she had it out of wedlock. Her family feel that the success of this plan depends on your help in the church and that your role should be to convince the people of the parish that she is to be treated like any-

one else. She asks to be reinstated as a Sunday school teacher.
How can you help this family most?

Such are the problems that come to the pastoral counselor in working with the unwed mother. Similar questions come to the parish
minister who has not even thought of himself in the specialized role
of counselor. Inasmuch as the people of the parish are involved in the
whole problem of out-of-wedlock pregnancy, they are involved in
the lives of the people who bring it home to them in their day-to-day
living. They depend on their pastor to see them through.

There will be times, however, when he may feel that he cannot
"see them through," because he is not sure what will happen next.
He is uncomfortable in the situation either with the unwed mother
or some member of her family. There will be occasions when the
unwed mother who has come to him for help refuses to accept his
suggestion that she needs immediate psychiatric help. Or it may be
her parents who resist the recommendation. The pastor may recognize that the girl is deeply depressed and may try to destroy herself,
or he may sense that her mental balance is precarious, and he fears
a psychotic episode. He may sense that the counseling process at
such a time especially destroys the defenses the girl has built up
over a long period of time. Without them, the present reality may be
more than she can endure. He cannot, therefore, withdraw the help
he has offered, for such action on his part may precipitate the feared
crisis. This is the time for him to remember that he does not have
to work alone. If he has not already done so, he can make himself
known to a qualified clinical psychologist or psychiatrist, present
his problem, and frankly admit his need for help. Many pastoral
counselors have already done this in connection with their general
counseling. The increasing number of pastoral counseling centers
have grown out of this kind of cooperation.

When the chaplain speaks to groups of clergymen about out-of-
wedlock pregnancy, specific questions usually follow the talk. Certain pastors seem to have more of one kind of out-of-wedlock situation to deal with than another. This would seem at first glance to
underscore the social causes of such pregnancy. But, then, two questions are raised: How much does the pastor of the church influence
social patterns? Is there something about the minister, himself, who

either attracts certain kinds of counseling situations or who handles counseling situations in such a way that the progress and outcome seem inevitable? While only a thorough research would provide the answer to these questions, nevertheless, the existence of these tendencies indicates that the pastoral counselor needs to think about his role both as a leader and as a counselor. The question we all need to ask ourselves is whether the contribution which we are making is a practical holding action, an effort toward a creative solution, or the beginning of a delayed housecleaning, or something of all three. The answer will depend upon one's theology of counseling, and upon the specific way it is related to the unwed mother, whom one must confront as Jesus did in his day.

CHAPTER SEVEN

The COUNSELING PROCESS BEGINS

Goals and Plans

The minister who is also a pastoral counselor must frequently examine the goals toward which he is striving. There is first the overall goal of his total ministry for which he was ordained. If he loses sight of this, his counseling will be aimless and either ineffectual or insincere.

Pastoral counseling has the goal of helping the counselee find and use his or her own strength so that fulfillment in the Christian sense is possible. The lay counselor, whether he is a psychiatrist, psychologist, or social worker, works with an unmarried mother to help her adjust to her social environment. It would be more appropriate for the professional counselor to include instruction in birth control in his program than for the pastoral counselor to do so. But the pastoral counselor has not finished his program until he helps his counselee see her behavior in a Christian context. The pastor and the unwed mother must both be aware that although he accepts her as a person, he does not necessarily condone her action.

The minister who counsels an unwed mother must also examine his goal as it relates to each counselee. For one girl, it may be to help her see herself as a person to be respected. For another girl, it may be to help her find a protective environment away from home where she can grow through feeling accepted and needed. For a third, it may be to help her see that her parents are people who need to be understood as much as she does. There are many specific goals to be spelled out.

Oftentimes, after a few sessions of counseling, there may come to light aspects of the counselee's problems that should change the immediate goals of the counselor. He should be able to reassess the situation and alter his direction if necessary. For instance, there may be a wide discrepancy between the picture of her family life as presented by the unwed mother in early interviews and the reality of the family relationships evident from later talks with other members of her family. Or, it may be that the situation regarding marriage to the father of the baby has been presented in one light by the pregnant girl and in quite another by her parents. The young man may or may not be the undependable, unstable, irresponsible, low, ugly character the parents believe him to be, or the misunderstood knight in shining armor that Bonnie thinks he is.

The counselor, seeking to deal realistically with their problems, will not accept emotionally-based judgments as factual information upon which sound plans can be formulated. The goal of social casework is to help the client to "change, adapt, and achieve." The goal of the clergyman is consistent with these aims, and he can therefore cooperate in whatever plans that are consistent with his ministry.

The plans of the pastoral counselor in cases of out-of-wedlock pregnancy are briefly as follows: allay the initial fears as soon as possible; present available resources; move toward problem-solving, drawing upon the *strength* of the counselee; help her by working with others involved in her situation as it seems necessary; provide follow-up support; help by having his parishioners, if need be, provide therapeutic fellowship.

Most of these six steps could be put into practice within one twelve-hour period or could cover a year or more. In any case, they should be thought of in this order, even though they may be used simultaneously. If the pastoral counselor panics and plunges into the middle of this sequence, he produces a short circuit more often than he produces a short cut, and someone gets burned.

Allay the Initial Fears

The emotional atmosphere of the first visit. Whether the unwed mother appears to be fearful or not, she has fears that are both specific and general. In most cases, her world has just collapsed and she is living a nightmare existence. Her mother, if the girl lives at home, may be experiencing fears that are just as terrifying. Most mothers fear for their daughter's physical welfare and her emotional state. Some fear their husband's reactions to the knowledge of their daughter's pregnancy and postpone telling him. Some dread the judgment of other close family members, who may imply that her daughter has failed them all. Those who have been taught that bearing an illegitimate child is THE unforgivable sin are both angry and afraid for both themselves and their daughters. They may feel hurt and personally wronged as well. When, therefore, both mother and daughter come together to see the pastor on the first visit, he will be conscious of the emotionally charged atmosphere surrounding them. Whether or not this tension will erupt, continue as the calm before the storm, or be denied both by mother and daughter will be determined by their characteristic way of meeting crises in their family.

No matter how they behave overtly, they are appealing for help at a time of great need. Since they are afraid and therefore less rational, the counselor's first job is to show them that life is not over for them, that there can be a bearable future for both of them. How is this done? It is primarily because the pastor feels that there is hope and forgiveness for them that he can be of help.

If the mother of a young pregnant girl brings her daughter to the counselor, it is not the daughter but the mother who will demand attention. The young girl will make herself as unobtrusive as possible, sullenly, tearfully, or fearfully. The first words of this mother may be, "I've warned her. I told her this would happen if she kept on as she's been going. But she wouldn't listen to me. She just kept on running around with that . . ." This mother's statement contains a large element of truth, unfortunately. The mother-daughter relationship was damaged long before the girl reached her adolescence, and she is but measuring up to the expectations of her parent. Too often, a girl acts out her parent's own unresolved problems through the power of suggested expectations. This mother needs help as much as her daughter.

Another opening remark of the mother may be: "How could she do this to me, after all I've done for her?" Two inferences can be drawn from such a statement: One is that the mother feels that the daughter purposely wished to hurt her (whose concern is for her own feelings and her own self-image). The second is that there should be some punishment meted out to her errant daughter.

What these disturbed mothers most need at this point is to feel that the counselor understands how *they* feel. They need to be assured that he knows that their daughters, whom they raised as best they could, have brought them grief. They need to feel that they have turned to someone who can help them practically as well as emotionally. Once the mother has been satisfied that she and her problem are understood, the counselor may ask for a few moments alone with the daughter, either during the first interview or at another convenient time. At that time, he can help the girl to express some of her feelings and learn what her expectations are apart from those of her parents. This is an important step before any plans are made, if a counseling relationship is to be established. More often than not, when the unwed mother is brought to the counselor, she will repeat what she has already said to her parents, "I want to make my own decisions." Her parents have already replied, "Look what happens when you do! You don't know yet what is best for you. When you show us that you can act like a responsible person, we'll be only too glad to let you make your own decisions." She, in turn, has complained, "How am I ever going to learn when it's always do this, do that." The foregoing conversation may take place in the pastor's office between mother and daughter on their first visit, or it may be repeated to him both by the girl in one private session, and by her parents at another.

If the unwed mother comes by herself, the pastoral counselor must keep in mind that any attempt to treat the whole problem at one fell swoop is to fall into the same trap into which the counselee has already fallen. She is swamped by the enormity and complexity of the problem as a whole.

The counselor will have accomplished much if he obtains basic information about the girl's situation by asking her matter-of-factly, "Have you told your parents?" "Have you been to a doctor to confirm this?" "When do you expect to deliver?" and "What about your young man?" These questions may stem the outburst or they may trigger the release of pent-up emotions, which the unwed mother has not yet dared to express. In either case, it is good and necessary that it be done. Furthermore, by these questions he can show his interest, his lack of shock or panic (which she probably expects him to feel), and his intention to be of whatever help he can. In most cases, he thereby allays her fears, builds confidence and establishes rapport.

The problems are multiple in out-of-wedlock pregnancy. They relate to medical care, family relationships, finances, social reactions, possible marriage, interrupted education, hiding the facts from relatives (younger brothers and sisters, grandparents who are old and ill and mustn't be given a shock, even from the children by a different father), holding a job, reintegration into the church, and future behavior and moral standards in this same world that contributed to this tragedy. These are some of the many problems that must be translated into questions and answers on which the girl and her pastor can work together.

Often the first time the pastor meets with an unwed mother in this kind of counseling relationship he will be surprised to have the unwed mother on leaving his office say what a help he has been and how much better she feels, even though he has done nothing at all to change her situation. She will come back, and he will have time to evaluate the situation in the meanwhile.

Another task of the pastor during this first visit is to determine the young woman's accessibility to therapeutic help, whether it be by himself or by another person. For instance, can she express herself verbally? Do her words actually relate to what she is doing and to the world about her? If not, as is sometimes the case (such a girl would not be able to respond to questions similar to those asked in the sample test cases), she needs a custodial situation in which to await her child. It is important to know whether or not she has the physical and psychical energy to make her own contribution to the help offered. If not, she needs medical and possibly psychiatric help under special conditions.

In this chapter, we have spoken of unwed mothers who have literally fled to their pastor for help in their panic. Presumably, these women considered that their pastor would offer them most help. We usually think of the unwed mother as having the same freedom of approach to counseling as anyone else. But is this always so? Is she as free to change her mind about going to a counselor at all as other people are when they have problems? This young woman is more or less pressured into "doing something," if not by the doctor, the family, the mate, or a friend, then by her own hopes and fears. We must realize that anyone sent or driven into counseling or therapy puts up a tremendous resistance either obviously or subtly. How much more, then, will the unwed mother offer resistance to the counseling which she voluntarily seeks?

Meeting resistance. It should be emphasized here that resistance wears more masks than Satan does. During the first visit of the unwed mother to her pastor, she may appear to be hungry for his advice and eager to cooperate; yet during the next half dozen visits, no progress is made. On the other hand, a girl may confront him in anger, as though he were personally to blame for all of society's prejudice and double-dealing, and leave him quietly grateful. Frequently, in counseling, what first appears to be may not be the case at all. In the following discussion of resistance on the part of the unwed mother, keep in mind that only the most common aspects with which the pastoral counselor may have to cope are used as examples.

Reasons for resistance. 1. As already mentioned, *the unmarried* mother is usually brought, sent or driven to the pastoral counselor. This is a sufficient basis for resistance.

2. The unwed mother, more often than not, *has never learned to trust people* and her first reaction to any helping person is that either he is doing it for some motive that she is not aware of or that it won't last. This has been her experience, or she feels that it has. She will, therefore, resist the very help she seeks, because she is afraid of being hurt again. This distrust, mixed with her fears, causes her to find enemies all about her, enemies that she has created. Uncertain about whether the pastor is an enemy or not, she will test him in many ways. Unfortunately, many of the unwed mother's enemies are more real than the Christian pastor cares to admit. He finds it difficult not to deny her charges of ill will on the part of people in whom

he has confidence. When he rushes to their defense, he aligns him-self with the enemy. He has to accept both her projections and her realistic evaluations without panic, if he is to build the kind of rapport he needs to help her subsequently to face a world in which there are both friends and enemies. Too often, friends would like to give the girl moral support, but they haven't the courage to do so. She may consider as enemies the following people:

Those who got her into this trouble;

Those who have betrayed her confidence;

Those who stand in the way of a marriage she hopes for;

Those who are ready to snatch the baby from her;

Those who would send her away from home;

The doctors who have performed all manner of indignities upon her (this includes even the most cursory examination);

Even God may be her enemy because he set up the rules which she has found "unfair," and because she now stands under judgment in a con-test that was rigged in the beginning.

3. The unwed mother may resist the help she seeks because she *emotionally denies* her pregnancy. She knows intellectually that she is going to have a child; her feeling is that there is an internal growth which must be removed before she can resume normal activi-ties. For her to talk about any plans involving the future of a child is so threatening to her that she will do almost anything to avoid it. The first visit is no time for such discussion. Often this girl wants to "go away for a while" and deliver her baby at a city hospital, release the baby to an agency immediately afterward, and then return home as soon as possible as though nothing had happened. Her mother will probably agree to this. However, when the baby is born, she may have an emotional reaction to this denial and suddenly change her plans. She may decide that she cannot and will not give up her child. Then, everyone who has helped with her earlier planning will become upset and unless they are experienced or naturally wise, they will try to influence her decision. Hence, the counselor encountering this kind of denial must be aware of the depth of the problem involved. When denial is part of the per-sonality pattern and is used to avoid any unpleasantness that threatens to destroy the illusion that all is well, it (like distrust) is of

long standing and is therefore a factor that caused the young, unmarried woman to become pregnant.

4. Another reason for an unwed mother's resistance to a pastoral counselor is that unconsciously she sees him as a figure of authority, against which she has rebelled in the past. If the young woman feels this way, then the pastor's role with this unmarried mother is little different from the counseling he offers youngsters in his youth group.

Any girl who becomes pregnant, not because she wants to be one of the gang, nor to be popular, nor to explore "life" and "live it up," but because she is psychologically predisposed to bear a child out of wedlock, will show great resistance because of her compulsion to act out her needs in this way.

The resistance of the young woman whose concern about her out-of-wedlock pregnancy is entirely of the practical considerations is not included in this list. This girl does not seek the minister for help; she knows he represents the ethics and morals which have little influence in her life and she doesn't wish to be "preached to." Perhaps, she may be a young woman studying at the university, where her lover may be doing postgraduate work. The two establish a way of life that permits sexual intercourse, but makes no provision for babies. Abortion is one solution, and failing this, adoption is another. A social agency will meet her needs. A minister cannot help her, for she does not wish to be helped by him. In the case of the delinquent, who has no previous or positive church experiences, the same considerations hold true. The pastoral counselor will probably not be confronted by her. Serving as a visiting minister to a local hospital or another type of institution, he may recognize this type of girl. In such a case, it is doubtful that the minister will see the unwed mother who rejects religion more than once in her brief stay at an institution. This is usually too short a time for a counseling relationship—but never too short for a miracle, although miracles have a way of evading busy schedules.

Mechanisms of resistance. The most obvious form of resistance (aside from walking out of the interview) is, of course, 1. *overt hostility* or anger. We all recognize this and react to it. We may

register annoyance, seek to better understand the counselee's behavior, or pretend the anger doesn't exist. This last response is as
unhealthy as the unprovoked anger that stimulated it. In fact, it is
the counselor's way of resisting the angry counselee! Immediate
anger on the part of the unwed mother may be the result of her
stereotyping the counselor as father, teacher, or judge advocate of a
punitive church or society. Her reaction is almost automatic. The
counselor's response to this initial skirmish will largely determine
whether he can help her or not. Her early display of brazenness
is usually a clue to how really frightened she is. She hopes to fool
you, and at the same time hopes that she will not. She challenges,
tests, and shocks you to predetermine the degree of acceptance and
self-confidence of the counselor. If you react with fear or rejection,
she doesn't need you. She already has her quota of fears. Her great
need is for strength and guidance.

When the pastor has such an angry cub in his study, he may say
to her:

Pastoral Counselor: Jody, you seem awfully mad at someone or some-
thing. Want to tell me about it before we go any further?
Jody: There's nothing to tell except I'm pregnant. I'm not going to get
married, and I'm sick of everyone telling me I've got to do this—do
that. I don't need any more opinions, I need answers.
P. C.: And you're afraid I'm going to give you opinions instead of
practical help?
Jody: Well, aren't you? Isn't that why you let me come?
P. C.: No. I hoped you'd come and talk it over.
Jody: Yah, talk it over—I've done that till I'm dry. Talk, talk, talk. I
want to *do* something.
P. C.: Well, like what?
Jody: I told you—Go away!
P. C.: Then let's explore the possibilities. Do you have something par-
ticular in mind?

At this point, Jody (and there are so many Jodys) may lay down
her cudgels and seek the help of the counselor.

2. *Withdrawal* is another form of resistance. The body and mind
are present, but the spirit is not. Such an unwed mother presents
herself to the minister, briefly relates her predicament, and then

stops. Thereafter, she answers his questions in monosyllables. This can be exasperating. Much patience is needed. He has no way of knowing whether he is getting through to her until she says, yes, no, or maybe, or until she requests another appointment. If she cannot accept his help, she simply will terminate the counseling sessions.

3. *Compliance* is a form of resistance seldom recognized by inexperienced counselors, because the counselee appears to be cooperative, sensible, insightful, and most of all appreciative and ready to pursue an agreed-upon course of action. The compliant girl can use as much or as little of your help as she chooses, while she leaves you feeling well rewarded for your trouble. When you carefully evaluate your work, you discover that the relationship was neither personal nor therapeutic. This unwed mother is a manipulator who long ago learned to take what she wanted and pay for it with ingratiating mannerisms. She believes that her world, and probably yours, too, are less painful this way. This is another girl with whom you need much patience. Someday, if she is fortunate, she may encounter someone who can help her face her basic deficiencies and help her rebuild her life on a more solid foundation. But this takes much skill and a long time. Her conscience is not a great help to her, and her charm is her enemy.

4. *Seduction* as a form of resistance is another problem for the pastoral counselor. It means that she may seek to use a smoke screen of personal magnetism to distort the real issues involved. When seductiveness is displayed as a form of resistance, the counselor has no choice but to confront the woman with her behavior and discuss what is taking place then and there.

5. *Intellectualization* is another form of resistance. At first you may think, "How refreshing it is to work with such an intelligent young woman." The young woman's gambit may be, "Well, here I am, a statistic, one of the 225,000 girls pregnant out of wedlock this year. Or has the figure gone up since Farrar's article came out last spring? I suppose I'm really a stereotype of the new unwed mother. You know, early twenties, girl next door, good family (here she lifts her eyebrows), good education, 'New Freedom,' I guess they call it—hmm—free from whom? That's my problem, Mr. Smith. Now

what do I do? Get rehabilitated, no doubt. I'm sorry if I'm offensive, but you can't imagine what this is like with everyone, but everyone, trying to give you advice when they simply don't know what they are talking about." This girl attempts to cover her emotions with talk, intelligent talk, because her self-image is that of an intelligent girl. She likes to think her head rules her heart, because she does not trust emotion. But she may shed a very unintellectual tear when her guard is down. One can accept her intelligence, while not being unduly impressed by it. The counselor is more interested in integrating both feeling and thinking so that they complement each other.

6. *Denial* is one of the most common forms of resistance. Unless, however, a girl is seriously disturbed, she probably does not deny the fact of her pregnancy. Rather, she acts the way most people do when they receive bad news: if they pretend it isn't there, it will go away. Society has, after all, encouraged this kind of denial. We offer anonymity in maternity and foster homes; we provide fictitious mailing addresses; we recommend early release of babies so that a girl can resume her normal activities as soon as possible. In other words, society also says, "Let's pretend it didn't happen." In this situation, we probably would suspect the mental health or emotional well-being of a present-day American girl, who does not deny the reality of her situation to some extent. The delinquent girl brags about her pregnancy as proof of her antisocial activity.

Not wearing maternity clothes even though physical appearance proclaims pregnancy, and not seeking help until it is almost too late to make good plans are examples of symptoms of denial. This type of unwed mother clings to the illusion that nothing has changed in her life. When she talks with her counselor, she avoids mention of the forthcoming child as long as possible, because she is not ready to look that far ahead. Allowing the baby to become a reality, even in her mind, means that many other painful realities must be faced as well. If the counselor forces her to face reality too abruptly, she will terminate her counseling sessions and seek help elsewhere.

The problem of denial is more serious when the unwed mother goes ahead and "makes plans" in her own mind and then acts as though these were workable. For instance, Ella says, "I'll go and stay with my friend, Sara, who has a house out in Meadowbrook. She has four little children. Her husband has something the matter with him so that he can't work much. So Sara has to go out to work sometimes. I can help out with the children and take care of Eddie when Sara is away." The counselor asks, "Have Sara and you talked this over?" "No," says Ella, "but it will work out fine. She told me last time I was there to come any time. She told me that there was always room for one more, even if she had to water the soup. I probably could take the baby there after he is born. I don't think it would make too much difference. When you are loyal friends, you help each other out." This conversation is but a brief part of that of a 28-year-old unwed mother, who, together with her baby, subsequently had to be given shelter in a city agency for homeless people. The friend, Sara, had enough problems with her alcoholic husband, and the watering of the soup was a daily occurrence. While this is an extreme case, there are many unmarried mothers who seek to deny reality by making unrealistic plans. Not only do these denials occur before the birth of the baby, but afterward, as just illustrated. The counselor who encounters it in the first visit may expect a recurrence in subsequent sessions. It is a problem that must be overcome with his help.

Denial is also at work when the unwed mother tells a story, often plausible, of "knock-out drops" and rape. The probability is that she was driven (unconsciously) into her predicament, and yet she finds her actions so abhorrent she must deny her part in it. For like reasons, a girl may claim that she became so intoxicated that she did not know what happened to her. She adds that she remembers "passing out," but that she does not remember a thing after that. Of course, the girl may be telling the truth. It takes long and skillful counseling to help this girl. In the meantime, she needs practical help and acceptance.

All of these kinds of resistance on the part of the unwed mother are evidence that it is painful for her to face the reality of the situation. The more forms the resistance assumes, the more threatening we may conjecture reality to be for her. If there is such a barrier of resistance, even though the unwed mother is driven to you by reality for practical help, you may be sure that her pregnancy is indeed the result of an emotional disturbance. This factor, which can be called the psychological dynamic of out-of-wedlock pregnancy, though it may not be great enough to warrant psychotherapy in all cases, certainly calls for competent counseling for the young mother after she has delivered her baby and returned to her community. In the meantime, the pastor should do what he can to help the unwed mother and her family to take care of the immediate needs of mother and child and to help them make plans in the most realistic way.

What takes place during the first visit?   In the first visit, whether there is resistance or not, the pastor should take the following steps: he should clarify the counselee's purpose in consulting him; outline his immediate procedure and purpose; and make plans for future visits. These things he does, both to organize his own thinking and to let his counselee know what to expect of him. Such a procedure reduces the chances of misunderstanding and facilitates the work to be done.

The counselor, of course, should make careful observations from the beginning. He should make note of defense mechanisms of the young woman, how frightened and uncomfortable she is (physical signs can often be observed), and just what role she thinks the counselor should play (father, God, society's avenger, ally, etc.). He should also be able to discern factual information from the distorted material he hears. If necessary he may conclude the first interview by informing the girl that he is not the one who can help. For example, the girl may be committed to a course of action that he cannot endorse, and for which she refuses to consider any alternative. She may be planning an elopement and quick marriage with an unsuitable partner, one who is not free to marry or who may be in trouble with the law, or may not be able to hold a job for more than a few weeks. Or, she may have made plans for her child which are neither in her best interest nor the baby's. She may have already arranged to release the baby to a friend of a friend, who agrees to pay the mother's expenses for delivering the baby to the baby's father's family or to the father and his new bride. Or, she may ask the pastor to be a party to a deceitful maneuver to "trap" or "punish" the baby's father or mislead her parents. If such an unwed mother refuses her pastor's invitation to discuss the matter with him further, she will probably leave and add him to her long list of disappointments. If, however, he can convince her that he accepts her in spite of their differences of opinion, she will make herself available and accessible for further help, and he will proceed as he would in any other case.

CHAPTER EIGHT

USING RESOURCES

While she is still stunned by the discovery that she is pregnant, the unwed mother usually has no clear idea of her present or future needs. She may turn to her pastor, hopeful that he will advise her at a time when she is utterly confused. On the other hand, she may go first to the doctor to confirm her pregnancy. She may think of getting married. If that is not possible or desirable, she may consider getting legal counsel. She may try to find a place to stay until the baby is born, and may seek information concerning baby adoption procedures. These initial gestures on the part of the unwed mother indicate the resources that she thinks she might need.

In this chapter, little needs to be said about the physician or obstetrician because knowledge of their services is known to the general public. While marriage as a resource to the unwed mother is frequently considered, it is less frequently chosen than it used to be. Adoption, as it relates to the unwed mother's plan for her baby, is presented from various points of view. In connection with adoption, a description of the various social agencies involved in such work is included. Maternity homes, their services and their availability, are described together with other prenatal facilities, such as foster homes and the hospitality of relatives. An adequate treatment of the legal aspects of out-of-wedlock pregnancy would require several volumes. Only those aspects of legal counseling that best serve the interest of all parties concerned are presented here.

Marriage. When the pregnant young girl goes to her pastor for help, she may hope that he will not only suggest marriage, but also that he will be able to persuade her boyfriend and both sets of parents that it is the best plan. She has no thought of further schooling either for herself or for her boyfriend, who may have plans for college. At the time, she may not think of their daily bread, but of their love nest with a healthy cooing baby, who is always dry and clean. Both sets of parents may be more realistic, however. They are usually angry with each other for having children who cannot be trusted to behave honorably. Most ministers today feel that if a marriage has already been planned and if in all probability it would have been a good one, then most likely pregnancy before marriage will not vitally alter the prospects of a successful marriage. The wedding can be moved forward to an earlier date. Only a minister knows how often this is done.

"Do these quick early marriages ever work out?" is a common and urgent question. There is evidence on both sides, but no actual statistics. One possible guide to the question of marriage of a pregnant young girl to her willing young man might be the answer to the following question: Would the marriage be a good thing for this couple if the woman were not pregnant? If the answer is no, the couple are too young or immature to marry were it not for the girl's pregnancy, then they are ill prepared for a marriage that begins with parenthood. If the answer is yes, then such a marriage may prove successful despite the out-of-wedlock pregnancy.

Here is a heartwarming example of the way one such marriage worked out. Not long ago a maternity home received a check for $200 as a "memorial to my dear wife who bore the first of our three beautiful daughters in your home over thirty years ago. Ours has been a wonderful life together. We hope through this gift to share in a small way in your ongoing program."

Adoption. We cannot compare statistically the number of unwed mothers who choose marriage for themselves and those who choose adoption for their babies, because we have only the adoption figures at hand. Only about 25 percent of the girls who are served by maternity homes keep their babies. It has been estimated that 29 percent of all the children born out of wedlock in 1960 were placed for adoption by 1961 (66,100)[1]. Unwed mothers may have placed their

---

[1] Adams and Gallagher, *op. cit.*, p. 46.

children for adoption for any of the following reasons: (1) they thought it was best for the baby; (2) they were advised or pressured to release the baby; (3) they did not think they could properly care for their baby; (4) they feared the stigma of illegitimacy; (5) they did not wish to be burdened by the responsibilities of motherhood at the time. Most pastoral counselors who volunteered information on this subject said frankly that they advised adoption for the babies of those unwed mothers who did not plan to marry at once. They advised this, because they had little evidence to believe that an unwed mother could successfully raise her child in the community, without incurring social sanctions.

The policies of social workers and agencies concerned with unwed mothers from the middle-class community vary. A large number of them advise release under almost all circumstances. Others believe it must be the unwed mother's own decision. They feel they serve the girl best if they help her explore her reasons for her decisions. Those who have long experience with unwed mothers know that some girls decide to *keep* their babies for good reasons while others release them for reasons which are just as sound. It is not the keeping or releasing that is right or wrong, but the reasons behind the choice. What is the possibility of making it work well for both mother and child? It may seem that a girl will wish to keep and raise her child because of her natural maternal instinct, whereas such a feeling may be a part of the basic needs that drove the girl to become pregnant. In one case, it may be the need to rebel against authority. In another, the child may be kept as a means of punishing either the unwed mother's family or the father of the child. A child kept for either of these reasons may at the same time be emotionally rejected by the mother. In such a case, she might "spoil" it with gifts and attention to cover her guilt.

A girl may return to her family with her child, because she and her family are at war with society. The new baby becomes an offensive weapon. The young woman who takes this stand may rationalize it in terms of "flesh and blood ties." Often, she is apt to criticize as unmotherly and heartless the girl who releases her baby for adoption. In another case, keeping the baby may symbolize the hope that marriage to the father is still a possibility. Sometimes, this action results in a baby remaining in foster homes for two, three or even more years until all hope of marriage is gone. Only then is the child released for adoption even though at such a time placement is more difficult, because the child is older. The demand for older children is not as great as for babies.

There are other reasons for keeping an illegitimately born child. As pointed out earlier, in some racial and ethnic or subcultural groups, illegitimacy does not bring shame upon either the mother or child. The baby is brought home, nurtured, and trained the same as the legitimately born child in a neighboring home.

There is no country that has such a high rate of adoption as the United States. It is not encouraged to such a great extent in Europe, although many children are born out of wedlock there. In many countries, the children are cared for by their mothers or relatives, who are helped by welfare assistance.

It should be reemphasized at this time that placing a child for adoption is one way that the unwed mother sometimes reduces her guilt. The adoption worker can work with the problems of psychological guilt. If the girl turns to her pastor, however, she needs his reassurances that she is doing what is right for her child. She will, in most instances, feel that God's forgiveness is mediated by her pastor.

The counselor will, no doubt, have some personal feelings concerning the mother's decision to keep or relinquish her baby, but they must not be allowed to interfere with the counseling process. The reason for this is not so much that he may advise her wrongly, but that by advising her at all, he may be denying her help at the deeper level of her personality problems. In the following examples, what on the surface seems to be a question of the pros and cons of releasing a baby for adoption is in actuality a matter of how the unwed mother meets her problems and how she relates to people.

The girl who has not yet learned that she must make her own decisions if she is to master the problems that arise from her situation will ask her pastor whether or not she should keep her baby. She may ask for his advice, because she knows intuitively that if he ventures an opinion or gives advice, he becomes personally involved in her problem. Indeed, some girls are very skillful at maneuvering people into such position, whereby they become entangled in her personal affairs and her life. These girls obtain emotional satisfaction from such a relationship, which proves to them that at least someone cares. The pastor, who reserves his opinions, will avoid this trap and aid the counselee to take her first independent step in problem-solving.

The unborn baby is often the focal point about which the pent-up feelings of both the unwed mother and her mother may be expressed. The counselor who injects an opinion at this point generally loses valuable opportunities for communication.

A most helpful procedure to follow in such situations is to refer the young woman and her parents to an adoption agency, a maternity home, or an agency whose first concern is for the welfare of the unwed mother and subsequently with her plans for the child. Such an agency has skilled caseworkers and consultants who can help a girl explore her feelings about her pregnancy and about the baby. When a girl finds that no one is going to *snatch* her baby from her, she may be able to make the altruistic gesture of giving up the baby for its own best good. Altruism is a maternal characteristic. When a girl is able to give up her baby on this basis, her femininity is increasing. An increase in femininity for the girl who has had inadequate feminine identification is a healthy step toward becoming a mature woman.

We recognize, however, that the element of needful punishment enters in as well. Only if the need for punishment is excessive is it harmful. One of the dynamics of this process of relinquishing the child is that if the caseworker who is working with the mother is different from the one who will be taking the baby, the unwed mother will frequently regard the first as her friend and the second as her enemy. Whoever actually takes the baby from her, even though she has arranged for this herself, runs the risk of becoming the emotional enemy, the child-snatcher. The wise counselor recognizes that the unwed mother's description of the adoption agency worker as a heartless, cold, inefficient, prying creature is her concept of anyone who separates her from her child. She is merely externalizing her inner conflict. Adoption workers are aware of this hostile transference and can work with it. When other persons who are trying to help the unwed mother with her problems get involved in child placement, issues and relationships usually get confused. It does not work well in the majority of cases, both for this reason and for the reason of lack of skill and knowledge on the part of those who are untrained in this field.

When it has been established that adoption is the best solution to the problem of the baby's welfare, the question of procedure arises. If the unwed mother is making plans for maternity home care, that agency will handle the adoption if it is licensed to do so, or it will have a direct working relationship with a qualified adoption agency. In either case, the unwed mother will have expert guidance and her rights will be protected.

If the unwed mother has talked with no one but her pastor about this plan to place her child for adoption, then it is her pastor who will put her in touch with a licensed adoption agency. Their case worker will help her to explore her real feelings about having this baby, will see her as soon as the baby is born, and help her not to panic if she experiences a change of attitude toward releasing the baby. Then, if the mother has not released the baby before leaving the hospital, she will place it in a reliable foster home until adoption plans are made. Any licensed adoption agency works according to state law, and the rights of both the baby's mother and the couple adopting him are guaranteed. If the unwed mother goes to the local family service association or child welfare bureau, they will, in turn, refer her to an adoption agency, provided they themselves do not serve in this capacity.

The unwed mother who goes directly to the out-patient clinic of a general or maternity hospital rather than to a family or welfare agency is usually referred to their social service department. There, she is requested not to leave the hospital until she makes practical plans for her baby's future. This prevents the abandoning of babies born illegitimately and also lessens the unwed mother's vulnerability to the black or gray marketeers. If she decides to release the baby for adoption, referral is made to an authorized adoption agency which assists her. The unwed mother can obtain help from a child welfare agency if she plans to keep her child, so that, if possible, she may prepare an adequate home for him. There is assistance available to the unwed mother for maintaining a family unit, which would per- haps be impossible otherwise. The pastor should know about the Aid to Dependent Children program in his area.

If an unwed mother accepts an offer of help from a doctor or law-yer to find an adoptive home for her baby, she may in some states be protected by state laws that refer all cases of adoption to a licensed or state agency. In some cases, she unwittingly delivers her baby to the gray market. It is not within the scope of this book to present the adoption laws of the fifty states, but the pastoral counselor is earnestly urged to learn exactly what the laws of his state are in this respect. More and more states are adopting legislation, advocated by the medical associations, that will prevent private adoptions. It is to be hoped that no minister will try to function as a matchmaker between babies born illegitimately and childless couples in his parish. He is as inadequately equipped for this work as the social worker is for conducting the Sunday worship service. However, Elizabeth G. Meier of Western Reserve University makes the following hopeful assertion. "Given the fact that the vast majority of babies are born with the potential for normal development and the likelihood that most people wishing to adopt a child have the capacity for parent-hood, the probabilities are that the majority of adoptions will work out reasonably well whether arranged independently or by agen-cies."[2]

Adoption as a resource for the unwed mother and the childless couple has proven to be a godsend. (It should not be forgotten, nevertheless, that in the ideal society there is little occasion for either.)

Prenatal facilities for the unmarried pregnant young woman vary. She may remain at home throughout her pregnancy, but this is not a likely choice for the girl who consults her pastor. After con-sulting her pastor, she usually decides to leave the community dur-ing the early months of her pregnancy so that any rumors of her pregnancy will be forgotten by the time she returns. She may go to stay with a relative. It is preferable for her to go to a maternity home, a foster home, or a recommended boarding home, where there are adequate clinical facilities, and qualified social case-work services nearby.

Medical care is a most important prenatal consideration for the

---

[2] Elizabeth G. Meier, "Independent Adoptions—Ten Years Later," *Children*, Volume 10, No. 6, (Nov.–Dec., 1963), p. 231.

pregnant young woman, married or unmarried. The younger she is, the more urgent is her need for care and instruction regarding her care. A private obstetrician or general practitioner can handle her case if she can afford it and plans to remain in the area. Moreover, an unmarried mother-to-be is just as welcome at the local hospital prenatal clinic as any other mother-to-be. The pastor will do what he can to encourage the unwed mother who comes to him to go immediately for a physical examination and then follow the doctor's orders regarding her health.

If the unwed mother decides to remain in her own home, which most of the unwed mothers who come to their pastor will not decide to do, she will make her medical and hospital arrangements and make the necessary arrangements with a local social agency if she plans to place her baby for adoption. If she plans to keep her baby, her whole family may need the services of a local social and family planning agency to help them adjust to the difficulties that in all probability lie ahead. The major difficulty occurs when family roles become confused; for instance, the grandmother may try to assume the care of both daughter and granddaughter. If the unwed mother plans to live alone or with a friend, she can usually avail herself of the services of a nurse from the Visiting Nurse Association, if her community has one, or of a former nurse or mothering person. Such people will be able to help her during the first difficult days of caring for her new baby. The pastor may be able to find help for her among the women of his church.

In some areas where unmarried girls keep their illegitimately born children, "baby showers" have been given for the young mothers by their friends. Pastors have been concerned lest such a procedure encourage illegitimacy. Our opinion is that premarital sexual promiscuity is encouraged where social rejection is the *only* deterrent. If premarital or generally promiscuous sexual relations are the norm and if the girls have no reason to value premarital chastity, then celebrating the arrival of a child born illegitimately will indeed be a stamp of approval or reward for such behavior. If, however, premarital sex experience is not condoned, it is not wrong for girls who feel compassion for the young woman who is pregnant out-of-wedlock and plans to keep her baby to make appropriate gifts individually or in small groups. It should not become a social occasion. It may be best for a wise adult whom the girls and young women respect to talk to them about this problem beforehand. The occasion, if properly handled, may prove to be a maturing experience for all concerned. The point to be emphasized here is that the baby shower should not be dealt with as an isolated event. It should be seen in the wider context of the unmarried mother. Nevertheless, it should be faced and used for a constructive purpose.

The maternity home,[3] as we have noted, provides aid for only ten percent of the prenatal arrangements of the unwed mothers. There are about 190 of these homes throughout the country, and they range in size from a house that accommodates a handful of girls to those that accommodate over 75 girls. They vary in standards and facilities, as they vary in function. Some facilities are entirely custodial. These keep the unwed mother in their care to guard her health, to keep her out of trouble, and to separate her from the community. The members of the staffs of these institutions consider that their function is more correctional than rehabilitative. This is not the usual pattern of the private social agency, such as those sponsored by the nondenominational Florence Crittenton Association of America, the Salvation Army, or most of the church sponsored homes. There are also a number of fine homes that operate independently, without profit. Some of these homes have hospital facilities within or adjoining the home. Others have arrangements with local hospitals, some for delivery and after-care; some just for delivery. In the latter case, the mother and child return by ambulance in a day or so to the home. Some homes are licensed to handle adoptions as well as offer maternity care. In such homes, there are facilities for infants as well. These homes, as other public facilities, are inspected by city health agencies and fire departments. Their appearance depends upon the interest and generosity of the supporting groups in the community. Some architecturally resemble a Charles Addams cartoon of a cobweb

---

[3] "A Directory of Maternity Homes" may be purchased from the National Association of Service to Unmarried Parents, 120 Grand St., White Plains, New York.

Gothic mansion, while others have the charm of a suburban private girls' school. Inside there are differences, of course.

The girl's ability to profit from her experience during her residence in the maternity home is not determined by its external appearance nor by the refinement of its decor. What makes the difference is the therapeutic milieu; that is, the warmth of the staff, the skill of the counselors and the girl's own ability to relate herself to those with whom she is living. One home says in its brochure that "it offers confidential counseling to both parents and makes every effort to help each girl make sound plans for her later adjustment to normal community life and a wise decision for the future of her baby." A school curriculum and specialists—including a psychiatrist, a clinical psychologist, chaplain and recreational leader—are available as part of the program. Medical care is directed by an obstetrician who is also a member of the staff of the local hospital where the residents go to deliver their children. Other homes still emphasize the learning of household skills and child care; a generation or so ago these lessons together with moral admonitions constituted the entire program, because all unwed mothers kept their babies. Most maternity homes, as well as most prospective residents, prefer that the unwed mother first visit the home for an interview and a tour of inspection before she makes final arrangements. If this is not possible, arrangements may be made by mail or telephone, often with the help of an experienced person (one familiar with institutional procedures of many kinds), to ease the anxiety of the girl and her family.

Most of these homes require a minimum residence of six weeks to two months. Girls may—are usually urged to—register early in their pregnancy and then come into residence when their condition becomes obvious or at the stated time. If a girl wishes to use the educational facilities of a maternity home, she will enter the home as soon as she leaves school. Otherwise, there will be a gap that cannot easily be filled by delayed tutoring.

Another facility offered by an increasing number of maternity homes is frequently called the family-plan program. As one home describes it, the plan has been developed "as an additional resource for some pregnant girls who would not benefit from a prolonged period in a group residence. 'Family homes' provide an opportunity for a girl to help with light household duties in exchange for an appropriate salary, and also to share in everyday healthy family life. A caseworker in the agency arranges and supervises these placements so that the plan is an integrated part of the total service."

Maternity homes have various rulings regarding how long an un-wed mother may or must remain in residence once she is released from the hospital. Where she does not see her baby and where the philosophy of the home is to return the mother as quickly as possible to her former way of life and shut off the entire experience of the maternity home as soon as possible, nothing is to be gained by con-tinuing her association with the home or its staff. In other homes, it is recommended that a girl remain three days to several weeks after the birth of her child to talk to her counselor about her baby, ter-minate her counseling if necessary, get her strength back, even find a job while still in a protective environment.

The cost of maternity home residence is a consideration, of course, but most homes, even those listed as private, are able to serve those who cannot pay because they have funds available from endow-ments, grants, or city, county, or state welfare allowances. The resi-dence fees vary geographically and according to the resources of the facility. Since admission is not determined by ability to pay for the service, people ask what are the criteria? The age, race, or creed of the unwed mothers are seldom considered relevant to admission procedures. The criteria are: (1) can the applicant benefit from the services offered by this home or should she be referred elsewhere? (2) will she be able to live with the other girls without disrupting the life of the home (because of emotional instability, behavior prob-lems, or precarious health, etc.)?

The pastor may be disappointed the first time he suggests a mater-nity home to an unwed mother. She may reject it immediately. This does not mean that she will not subsequently reconsider her decision when she finds it is not "just a way to get rid of her" or that she is not being sent to the home as a punishment. He may be surprised when she objects on the grounds that she would be unhappy living under the same roof with "that kind of girl." Many girls are surprised upon their arrival at the home to discover that there are no bars on the windows and that most of the girls they meet are rather like their friends at home. Frequently, a girl is uncertain about applying for admission to the home when she visits it for her interview. There seems to be a finality about it which is frightening to her. Then too, she may be unready to identify with a houseful of girls, all wearing maternity clothes and obviously pregnant. For the girl who is not ready to face reality, this is too threatening. Yet, this very facing up to objective reality helps her to accept her own position. To be aware of these dynamics is to be prepared to help the unwed mother more skillfully than merely pointing out the resources and saying, "Well, what'll it be?"

Some girls may prefer to stay with a relative until they go to the hospital for delivery. Her parents may suggest such a solution in the interest of economy as well as out of conviction that their daughter will be in better hands than if she were with "strangers." It would be wrong to claim that this system never works. We do not have statistics. But if it is to be made to work, the unwed mother will need social casework as though she were at home or in a maternity home. Not only does the girl take her problems with her, but she adds to them, for she lives in a home where she is not a guest, a member of the family, a boarder, or a charge. Her habits are not always those of her relatives, and this in itself becomes a source of friction over the course of several months. The young unwed mother does not usually feel free to mix socially with local contemporaries, whom she may not know, and she may be easily bored with the adults who are more like her parents than she thought they would be. Under such conditions, a girl can become as depressed as if she were living alone in a rented room. Often, her hosting relatives become frustrated and think her either ungrateful or peculiar. Some girls change their plans abruptly when things come to this state. Some apply to a maternity home and some return home where the frustrations and tensions are at least familiar and therefore more bearable.

There is another danger inherent in this kind of arrangement. Even though both parents and their relatives may enter into such an arrangement for the girl with a sense of cheerful confidence, both parties, in time, become irritated about imagined wrongs, failure to agree on certain procedures, and many other things. One may seem bossy, one feels obligated, one keeps too careful account of expenses, one condescends, one has no discipline; there is no end to the complaints. The agitation increases as the letters fly back and forth. Only strong character can overcome the inherent problems that arise from such an arrangement. It can be done, of course, especially if all parties involved have help. The pastors of their churches, who will understand their predicament and be able to guide them, may shift the balance from failure to success.

Foster home placement for young unwed mothers is a plan utilized by social agencies that either do not have maternity homes available or that have worked on this plan by choice. When a girl is ready to leave her community or when she must leave a home which may prove injurious to her present health and future welfare, then the caseworker takes her to a carefully selected home where understanding foster parents make her welcome. They may provide healthful family living in a manner entirely new to her. Such an example may have a definite therapeutic effect on her outlook and adjustment, both present and future. The social worker continues to visit her in the foster home and help her with plans for herself and the baby. If the unwed mother is very young, say under fifteen, this foster home plan has many advantages, not the least of which, in cases of previous destructive home environment, may be the invitation to return there for a longer period of time. The minister can easily find out if such a plan is available in his area, and he is urged to do so.

Selected boarding homes are recommended by some agencies for unmarried pregnant women. While these are not supervised as foster homes are, they are selected because they provide a good environment for the more mature girl. Here also, the social worker should be available to the unwed mother to help her make plans.

Such then are the *prenatal facilities* that are available to the unmarried mother. There is no need today for any unwed mother who is in contact with the community around her to go through her pregnancy without help and hope. Yet, many do so, for they are either ignorant of or else feel embarrassed and shy to accept the many services that are available to them. We should like to be able to say that the arrangements we have described always prove satisfactory to residents and their parents. But this is not true any more than it is true that all patients are satisfied with the same hospital facilities. As long as there are round and square pegs and round and square holes, there will be some ill-fitting accommodations.

Legal counsel can benefit the unwed mother in more ways than by suing the putative father of the baby for her expenses and for the baby's support for the next 21 years. There are those people who believe, either because they have been told by "someone who knew someone who" or because they have actually had a bad experience, that it is a common practice for girls pregnant out of wedlock to point a finger at a prominent man and say, "He is the father of my child." Whereupon, these people say, the poor man has to pay a fortune to settle the case even though he is not the father. On a radio program not too long ago, this point of view was presented and listeners responded with telephone calls sympathizing with this misuse of the courts of justice to perpetrate a fraudulent practice. We know hundreds of girls who have never gone to a lawyer for help in meeting even part of their expenses. In all fairness, one would have to admit that both situations exist. In areas where prominent and colorful characters attract those who prey on their fame or fortune, one will find more fraudulent claims. On the other hand, in suburbia, especially, the last thing the unwed mother wants is publicity. She is often afraid to go to court with a just claim, because someone might hear of it. In many cases, no redress is sought by the unwed mother because any tie, even financial, to the erstwhile mate is distasteful once he has denied responsibility. To sue is too humiliating for many girls.

Just as many questions have arisen in your mind as you read the previous paragraph, so questions come to the mind of all of those concerned in a case of out-of-wedlock pregnancy. Guessing at the answers can cause grief, if one acts as though the guess were correct. When someone shouts, "I'll have you in jail for this," it is a brave or canny soul that does not quake. When it is shouted at Greta's young boyfriend by Greta's father, both families should know their legal rights. When, on the other hand, Rocky tells the unwed mother of his child that she cannot place it for adoption, that his parents will take it away from her, what are the rights of the mother, of Rocky, and his parents?

A young mother named Melody has settled for $1,000 as expenses to care for herself and for the baby in a foster home until she signs the release for the adoption. The baby's young father and his parents are relieved that it cost them no more. Now, they can send him back to college. Then comes the blow. Melody decides to keep her baby and raise her. She applies for Aid to Dependent Children and is told she cannot obtain it as long as the father of the child can be found and made to support her. When informed of this, the paternal grandparents scoff at the idea. They state, "A settlement has been made for $1,000. You have no further claim on us." What are the legal rights of all concerned? Will the grandparents be forced to pay additional money for the support of the child despite the fact that Melody had agreed to accept the $1,000 as full payment?

Another girl, Linda, decided to keep her baby and planned to have her name and her baby's name legally changed from Chacovsky to Miller—the name of the man she claimed was the baby's father. She planned to return to the town in which both the Chacovskys and the Millers lived. The Millers said they would fight; the Chacovskys said, "Go ahead." What would a judge say about the change of names?

To return to situations in which there seems to be a legitimate need for legal advice, the following remarks by Ruth L. Crowley, Assistant Attorney General of the State of Maine, seem to sum up well the place of the legal profession in cases of out-of-wedlock pregnancy.[4]

The attorney might be of greatest professional assistance to unmarried parents and their children in four respects. These are:

1. Rendering legal counsel to the unmarried mother to interpret her legal rights concerning her illegitimate child.

[4] Excerpts from "The Attorney's Role in Services to Unmarried Parents and Their Children," a paper delivered on September 6, 1963, in Sharon, Mass., by Ruth L. Crowley, Assistant Attorney General, State of Maine, at the Third Annual All-Day Workshop held under the auspices of the Booth Memorial Maternity Home of the Salvation Army.

2. Representing the mother in a judicial determination of paternity of a child born out of wedlock—that is, in the ugly, legally designated bastardy proceedings.
3. Representing the accused father in such bastardy proceedings.
4. Representing the adopting parents, if the child of unmarried parents is to be adopted.

Time does not here permit a comprehensive discussion of all these aspects of the attorney's role in services to unmarried parents and their children, but I will very briefly mention some of the commonest aspects of each of these roles. Unfortunately, most mothers of children born out of wedlock do not seek legal counsel concerning their rights to these children and are frequently in fear or shame, misguided legally by persons not qualified to interpret these rights. By law, legitimacy is regarded to be a matter of legal status. There is a vast difference between a statute which provides for inheritance rights to be given to a natural child who is formally recognized by his parents and a statute which provides for the legitimation of a child. Many states have legal provisions for rights of inheritance and support by an illegitimate child from his natural father, but unless that child is legitimated by a method legally accepted in a given state, then the social status of that child is unchanged; he is still illegitimate and not uncommonly frowned upon by the so-called "best society."

For various reasons many fathers are unwilling to formally acknowledge or legitimate their illegitimate children. In such cases, if the mother wishes to establish paternity—which, in the absence of meeting other statutory provisions does not legitimate a child—then she must institute bastardy proceedings. If successful in her action, she will be able to enforce support of the illegitimate child during its minority by its legally adjudicated father. The legal format of bastardy proceedings varies from jurisdiction to jurisdiction, but typically it resembles a criminal action while in substance and effect it is a civil action. It should be noted that bastardy proceedings are not popular because such proceedings necessitate the use of evidence which identifies much socially unacceptable conduct on the part of both the mother and the putative father.

Statistics show that a large number of children born out of wedlock are released for adoption. Again legislation in this field varies greatly in different states. Generally, state statutes require the consent of the mother only for the release of an illegitimate child. Adoption proceedings are wholly a matter of statute, since this right to release one's child to another person or persons did not exist at common law. Inheritance rights are closely intertwined with adoption proceedings, with some states allowing inheritance from only the adopting parents and others, like my own state of Maine, giving the adopted illegitimate child a premium inheritance from both its natural mother and its adoptive parents. An unwed mother who releases her child for adoption needs legal counsel as to her rights and the termination of same. Only an attorney is qualified to spell out and interpret these rights to her.

Most of us are aware that certain general principles exist, but we must also remember that the specifics can make the difference. For instance, any man having sexual intercourse with a girl under a certain age may be imprisoned for statutory rape. If the young man were your son, or the president of your youth group and the girl were the 16-year-old junior-class president, it would make a big difference to you whether the law of your state set that certain age at 14, 15, 16, 17, or 18!

Another example may be cited. A girl that comes to you for help wants to place her baby for adoption despite her mother's opposition to the plan. You encourage her proposal because you come to the conclusion it is in the best interests of both the girl and the baby. You assume that she has the legal right to do this, because a similar situation occurred in another state where your last parish was. Then you learn that in your present state a minor must have the parent's or guardian's consent. We could go on in this vein endlessly, but more will be gained if the pastor spends his time talking to an attorney in his parish or community or inquiring about legal services available to people with more need than resources.

Although this chapter has been devoted to the resources available to the unwed mother, we mention again the *help available to the pastor* when he feels uncomfortable in the counseling situation. This is part of the team approach that we have been stressing in our work with the unwed mother. The staffs of many of the agencies mentioned in this chapter, as well as pastoral counseling centers, have consultant psychiatrists to whom they turn when a problem warrants it. The pastoral counselor should not overlook the psychiatrist in his community as a resource for his client and for himself.

CHAPTER NINE

The COUNSELING PROCESS CONTINUES

Once the counselor has allayed the initial fear of the unwed mother and has introduced the available resources to her, the decision must be made whether this counseling relationship will be continued or not. If the girl is going to leave the community as soon as possible, there will be little opportunity for the sessions to continue. However, the pastor can "keep the door open" until she returns. One way he may do this is to ask the woman's permission to visit her, if possible, wherever she plans to live. Most girls are proud to have their ministers from home call upon them. However, while she is away from home, there may be a skilled caseworker from a qualified agency who will assume the counseling role and help her to work through many of her practical and psychological problems. There also may be a local chaplain or clergyman whom she can consult if necessary.

Guilt and forgiveness. It may not be until after the parents and daughter have made whatever practical arrangements seem appropriate that they will be ready to cope with their feelings of guilt. The girl herself may do this while she is away or after she returns home. However, her parents—and occasionally her young lover—are fortunate if they can go to their pastor and discuss such feeling with him. It is not easy to bring to light those things which have been so long hidden and which are deeply humiliating. The counselor is not surprised to find that the counselee avoids the subject and prefers to talk about more mundune affairs. If guilt were not so painful, people would not so persistently avoid facing it. The parents of the unwed mother find it easier to bemoan their guilt in a general way rather than be specific and say, "This I will do to make amends." It has been the experience of many counselors for parents to ask them earnestly, "What have I done wrong?" By selective listening, they manage never to hear the true answers. Parents usually feel that they both loved and showed their love to their daughter in every way possible and that consequently there must have been some mysterious force at work in their daughter's life which interfered with the natural or logical effect of their love on her character. Parents will often make the statement that what happened to their daughter could happen to anyone, or that everyone is apt to make some mistakes in his life. These remarks seem to reflect a nonjudgmental attitude, but may instead be an effort to reduce the self-judgment that produces feelings of guilt. As a pastoral counselor, one should be ready to explore all the highways and byways of a parent's thoughts as well as those of the unwed mother. It is usually easier to approach guilt obliquely.

Practically all pastoral counselors have heard a father of adolescents or teen-agers say, "Of course, I was no saint myself. But no one can say that I ever shirked my responsibility. Why, I've even been working at two jobs to give Barbara and the other kids a good home and a good education. I just don't understand it. We've taught them right from wrong and we've trusted them. What more can we do? Frankly, my wife's just about at the end of her rope, and I just don't know."

The pastor will seek to help such a parent honestly to forgive his daughter, for only by his learning how to forgive one who has hurt him deeply, can he experience forgiveness himself. If the pastor feels compassion for the burden of guilt from which his counselee suffers, if he accepts that person regardless of what he has done or how unworthy he may consider himself to be, and if he believes that God will indeed forgive a repentant sinner, then a young woman or parent that seeks aid from this pastor will come away convinced that she or he has received help. The *atmosphere of faith* and trust in the ever-present God is essential to such a session regardless of the words spoken. One assumes, of course, that the words are not in contradiction to the atmosphere. On the other hand, as every counselor knows, the cleverest or most beautiful words cannot comfort the man or woman who senses that the counselor is his own god. The pastor will, of course, ultimately deal with the guilt of his counselee according to his own theological interpretation. Only when he has helped the unwed mother or her parents separate their guilt from their "problems" will he be able to help them understand and experience redemption and forgiveness.

A minister was confronted by the mother of an unwed pregnant girl. The family had finally made plans acceptable to all concerned, and they should have been relieved. But Mrs. Ecks was still troubled. She told her pastor that she felt guilty, but she didn't know what she had done wrong. Instead of feeling that she should go to church and find solace in prayer, confessions, and Holy Communion, she felt too unworthy to enter the sanctuary. What should she do? Her pastor replied, "Well, I guess you had better stay out of the church until you can find what you have done wrong. Return home and pray about it. When you are ready to make your confession, you will be able to return to church." This was one minister's application of his theology to this problem. One feels he might at least have recommended some Psalms without compromising his position. The penitential Psalms have helped many an unwed mother through her physical and spiritual agonies.

As the pastor must help the woman resolve her guilt, so must he also help the family of the unwed mother in their need to be forgiven. Often, young women and their families feel that they are fulfilling our Lord's requirements for forgiving others when they say that they no longer find out-of-wedlock pregnancy unforgivable and that they themselves will never again pass judgment on a girl pregnant out of wedlock—unless, of course, she is brazen and unrepentant about it. However, these same girls may add, "Even though I know God can forgive me, I can't forgive myself, so I still feel unforgiven. I know, I can't expect to feel God's forgiveness until I forgive myself." It is said over and over again by girls in maternity homes when they gather together in church-sponsored groups for discussions of this very kind. These remarks also echo the dormitory laments of girls who cannot sleep because of their spiritual unrest.

What frequently happens, it seems, is that the girl who consults her pastor at the beginning of her pregnancy about the sense of guilt and shame is assured by him of God's forgiving love. Hopefully, she assumes that it is only a matter of time before this assurance becomes a reality to her. Then she leaves home before there is further opportunity to explore the full dynamic of forgiveness. Perhaps when the girl returns to her parish still feeling unforgiven, her pastor can help her see that forgiveness cannot be related to only one area of living, such as out-of-wedlock pregnancy. The girl who comes to feel that she can forgive another unwed mother has yet to learn that the judgment on which forgiveness is based is reserved for the Lord God, not for us. For her to forgive the sins of those who have not sinned against her is her way of hopefully deferring judgment against herself. Selecting errors and sins for which she can feel forgiveness is yet another mechanism which gets in the way of her own experience of forgiveness. She also has as much trouble as anyone in the parish with the concept of resentment as a block to forgiveness. It is resentment in particular that stands in her way to forgive her parents. She projects her resentment to them and from them to God. Thus, she soon begins to believe that there is no forgiveness either from them or herself. Her family usually can't help her with this problem, because they share it.

Counselors from the other professions, while they recognize the problem of guilt, do not treat it as a religious problem.

If the young mother feels that giving her baby up compounds the guilt she already feels about her sexual activities, getting pregnant, betraying the trust of her parents and friends, placing her family in an embarrassing position, making it necessary for them to tell lies, telling lies herself about her whereabouts, then no amount of persuasion on the minister's part will reduce her guilt feelings in this one respect. She will need more counseling before she will be free to experience forgiveness at any level, by God, by her family, or by herself.

Self-image. Guilt, forgiveness. These are religious matters obviously. But there is another matter which the religious counselor may not think of as being specifically religious, that is, the *self-image* of man, any man. It is hard for anyone suffering so much from feelings of guilt, from the feeling that God hasn't yet or can't forgive him, to accept the scriptural statement that "God created man in his own image, in the image of God he created man; male and female he created them." In what possible way could such a person bear the image of God his creator? As one girl said, "That image must be buried very deep in most of us. I haven't seen it yet!" That girl's idea of both herself and other people was not a lovely one. As mentioned earlier, a low self-image, a low opinion of one's own values, is a characteristic of many unwed mothers. Overcompensation may result in an attitude of conceit or self-inflation. When this self is deflated in spite of every attempt to protect it, the girl becomes depressed and finds no comfort in a religion that seems so contradictory to experience.

Here are a few of the questions which have perplexed unwed mothers who have had Sunday school, youth fellowship, or church backgrounds. "If God made man in his own image, why did the first man and first woman sin right away?" "Why the need for the Commandments if we are made in God's image?" "If Jesus took away our sin when he died, then we won't be punished for this (getting pregnant out of wedlock)! But shouldn't we be punished just the same, so we won't do it again?"

In a letter, an unwed mother wrote to her pastor the following words: "We are not made in God's image. He is righteous; we are not even decent. He is spiritual; we are flesh and blood and are stuck with it until we die. Some of us are females, but God is always He. I don't get it." These are the words of a young rebel who felt guilty, who hated being a woman, who wanted to be someone even though she felt like no one. Part of her problem, of course, was related to her low regard for her own sex. But as the pastor worked with her, he accepted her as a human being, not as a family problem or a "case." He helped her to see herself in a different light, as a woman who was going to have a child, and as an individual who had many good qualities and strengths on which to build. She was able to make positive plans for her baby and for her own future, which she had not been able to do before. With this foundation, the pastor helped her replace her immature religious concepts with a belief and faith that was relevant to her total life. Not the words the pastor used in this situation, but the total impact of his attitude and his sensitivity to her needs and her potential redeemed her self-image. And within her, she discovered a reflection of the Creator. Needless to say, this pastor and the unwed mother were willing to continue the counseling long after the initial crisis was past.

Another case illustrates the importance of using whatever strength there is, especially when the self-opinion is low. At sixteen, Elthea was a ward of the state. She had been in eight foster homes in her short life and was aware that she had brothers and sisters, but had never seen them. The home where she lived when she became pregnant was the happiest she had known, and she called the foster parents Mother and Father. She wanted to drop out of school the year before her pregnancy occurred, but she continued her education to please her foster parents. The school authorities felt her performance was below her ability, but Elthea was sure she was stupid. At the maternity home, she got along well, helped out whenever asked, and did well what she was asked to do. When anyone noticed this and suggested she do something more complicated or take any responsibility, she either made an obvious mistake (as though to prove her inability to function well) or she dropped out of whatever group asked her to assume responsibility. She expected, quite unrealistically, that she would return to her foster home with her baby. When it was pointed out to her that she could not do this, she said she would get a room, find work, and support her child. At first, she refused to see how impossible this would be for her because of her age. She said repeatedly, "This is my baby, *mine*. No one can take him away. He's all I have. I won't give him up. He's my own flesh and blood, part of me. He's my only blood relation. I'll take care of him somehow." Elthea was determined to take care of her child. Where was the strength to be found that she needed? Her low self-opinion had to be raised if she was to think of herself as a mother. She began to see herself as a mother planning for her child. She returned to the foster home to finish her schooling along more practical lines. Her baby was cared for in another foster home where she could visit him. She began to get better marks in all subjects, and to consider school as something that might prove useful to her future life. She also showed a sense of responsibility about many things she avoided before, because for the sake of her child she was less afraid to fail than she was of not trying.

The final notes on Elthea's progress show that she finished school, got a job, and lived with her small son in a home, where he was taken care of afternoons while Elthea worked. They were a happy and loving mother and child at that time. The image of God in this young woman was indeed hidden until with skillful help, she gained self-respect, accepted responsibility, and gave rather than sought love. In the beginning, she had attended church because she was told to. It meant little other than pleasing someone. When she took her son to live with her, she asked to have him baptized in the church she was attending. The pastor commented that for such a young mother she seemed to have a great deal of maternal instinct and pride, and enough faith for the two of them to last a long time.

In addition to helping the unwed mother with her spiritual problems, the pastoral counselor can help her change some of her immature motivations. He can help her find her own strengths and talents so that her life need not always be subject to whims or seem to be determined by a grim fate. In the case of out-of-wedlock pregnancy, as in any other pastoral counseling situation, if the counselor observes that nothing he has to offer is going to help the girl or her family, he can then only hope that they will find other help—which he may recommend—or that he can simply be available to them as wisdom dictates. He need not feel that he has failed them.

Postnatal reactions.   If the pastor has made it plain before the unwed mother went away that he would like to see her when she returns, or if he has seen her in the meanwhile, then she will probably go to him soon after her baby is born. This is a critical time for her. The birth of her child has aroused many emotions within her that must be faced honestly. The disposition of her baby will raise reactions which must be well handled if they are to be finally laid to rest and not merely repressed. It is important that the counselor learn whether the mother considers giving up her child as a form of atonement or punishment. It is equally important for him to know whether the pleasure of keeping the child includes a willingness on her part to face years of unselfish nurture, or whether it represents the victory of possession. Will the child be used as a means of inflicting punishment on herself, her parents, or even the child. Although plans were made before the baby was born, postnatal developments may threaten to upset them. The pastoral counselor can use this period to help the unwed mother and her parents grow in understanding and love toward one another.

There are families, as well as social agencies or professional advisors, who advise a young woman to forget the entire experience of out-of-wedlock pregnancy. Yet, we believe she usually needs someone with whom she can talk about her experience and about her child a little longer. The pastor can make it possible for her to release some of the tension that denial builds up. It is much better for the unwed mother to talk with her pastor than to confide in a friend whose interest stems from curiosity or vicarious pleasure and who may betray the confidence.

When an unwed mother returns home after giving up her child for adoption, she may want to tell her parents about her experience of becoming a mother, about the baby's appearance, and about the sorrow of giving it up. Because her mother and father have their own problems regarding this out-of-wedlock pregnancy, they may be unwilling to listen or discuss anything concerning the baby—their grandchild. They may rationalize that such discussion is unwise or they may complain that it is unfair to put them through such an emotional ordeal. When the parents refuse to share their daughter's feelings, the emotional rift between them widens. The pastor, if he is aware of this, must try to help the parents to receive their daughter's confidence, or failing that, can make himself available to listen if she still needs to talk about what she has been through.

Special cases. This chapter on the counseling process would not be complete without mention of special cases, that have been met by other pastoral counselors and those which the reader may be confronted with at any time. How does one help the mother whose baby is malformed? The mother whose baby is unadoptable?

The girl whose baby is stillborn may either be grief-stricken or euphoric. In either case, the first need is the doctor's explanation of what happened. The unwed mother may believe that the stillbirth is part of God's plan either to punish her for her sin or to spare the baby future unhappiness or misfortune. Her own pastor will know best how to help her meet such a crisis so that she may gain insight, maturity, and spiritual growth. The important thing on such an occasion is that the girl be counseled in a way that is not incompatible with her total religious beliefs.

For example, there was Bonnie. The hospital chaplain visited her when she was informed that her baby died at birth. "I have killed my child," she wailed. "I tried to get rid of it when I first got pregnant, and it didn't come. Then I got used to the idea, and lately I've been looking forward to having my baby, my very own baby, and I killed her. It is God's way of punishing me for all I've done, isn't it?" The chaplain managed to quiet Bonnie's almost hysterical crying and prayed:

> O Living Lord, who art with us at all times, to whom we can turn in times of crisis, give us the comfort of thy presence now and give us quiet mind and heart that we may understand the meaning of this tragedy. As thou dost love the little one scarce born who is now at thy side, so love us who remain to mourn. We ask this in thy holy and loving name. Amen.

This prayer for quietness of mind and understanding served to prepare the girl to listen to the explanation by the doctor. The chaplain then had a heart-to-heart talk with the frightened and grieving young mother. No references were made to causes, to punishment, to anything but the Lord's care for both mother and child.

The hospital chaplain does not know the theological position of his patient, nor is that important. The chaplain will urge her to talk this over with her pastor but if she has not told him of her pregnancy, she will probably not tell him this either. In their brief time together, the chaplain may not be able to dispel the mother's anger nor change her belief about what she regards as God's purpose for what has happened. Yet, he may share her grief and offer his consolation to her.

There are various procedures in different hospitals regarding funerals for babies who are stillborn or die after birth. The patient may request that the chaplain be allowed to read a funeral service.

On the other hand, she may turn the funeral arrangements over to the hospital.

If Bonnie's baby had been malformed, her reaction would probably have been intensified. Because of the guilt the unwed mother feels anyway, she is more often than not afraid that her child will be deformed, misshapen, incomplete, brain-damaged, or mongoloid. Her first words usually are, "Is he all right?" and when she holds him for the first time, she examines him minutely and relaxes only after she finds normal feet, hands, head and body. Occasionally, she has to be told of a heart murmur or other congenital defect. When this happens, the doctors and nurses usually perform their service well, but it is to the pastor that the young woman must turn for further help. If the pastor believes that God is indeed punishing the woman for her sexual sins, then he must be sure that he helps her to atone so that she may be forgiven, or she will have a burden greater than she can carry. One meets such people in mental hospitals.

In contrast to Bonnie, Lilla's baby died several days before the mother delivered. She was aware that all movement had ceased and reported this to the nurse at the clinic. She was examined and was told to be ready to go to the hospital. When the doctors said the baby had been dead several days, she was not surprised. Instead of grief she expressed joy over God's wonderful providence in giving her child a heavenly home. "God was so good to me," she said. The chaplain knew that she would not tell her pastor at home of her feelings, because her mother had forbade her telling him. The chaplain offered prayer in this manner:

O most merciful Father, we turn to thee now in both grief and thanksgiving. We grieve over the loss of this little one to whom life could have been a joy as it is meant to be for all thy children, but we are thankful that all of us are destined to be with thee through all eternity, where earthly ills are past and the treasure of heaven is present. For all thy blessings to us and to all people we praise thee O Lord. Amen.

The chaplain then told her he hoped that the experience would prove a maturing and creative one for her, when she gave thought to it in the future. This last he added hoping that Lilla would not repress this immediately and refuse the reality of it as her euphoria seemed to indicate she might do. Her guilt, unlike Bonnie's, was too threatening for her to face.

How does one help the mother whose baby is unadoptable? There is no easy answer, or no one answer to this question. If the unwed mother plans to place her child for adoption, she, no doubt, will try to arrange the matter with a social agency. The social worker that handles her case will become aware of the baby's unadoptability, for she will learn this fact from the woman's doctor. When the unwed mother is told, she will react in one of several ways. She may say, as one girl did, "Well, I couldn't have taken care of him either if he has to be institutionalized. I'll just have to release him to the state."

As time went on, she grew more and more angry with the adoption worker for not finding a permanent home for her daughter. She attributed this failure to the social worker's "lack of interest" in her child and to "people's racial prejudice." Her minister was not able to break through this wall of guilt and hostility. Figures are not available for the children born out of wedlock to unwed mothers who are of a different race from the baby's father. Some children are kept and brought up by the mother; some are brought up by the parents who subsequently marry; some are placed in foster homes, usually of people of the baby's obvious coloring; and some are released to the state, with the hope that through the efforts of a specialized agency[1] a home may be found for the child.

There was a baby born a few years ago to a young unwed mother who planned to place it for adoption at the request of her socially prominent and wealthy parents. They could see no place in their plans for themselves or their plans for their daughter for a baby born out of wedlock. When the baby arrived, it was found to be malformed, not enough to endanger its life but enough to preclude a "normal" life. The parents continued to think in terms of giving up the baby even though it could not be adopted and would have to be institutionalized. The unwed mother's reaction was "I have

---

[1] For instance, in Massachusetts, the Division of Child Guardianship has a Family Recruitment Project to "find adoptive parents for children."

wanted to keep my baby since I knew I was pregnant but agreed to give him up because I felt he would have a good home with both a mother *and* a father. It is different now. I shall keep him with me even without a father. I think I am glad it came out this way, not that he should be crippled but that I have no choice." The new grandparents stormed, wept, and threatened, but the girl stood on her right to keep and support him. She was finally allowed to bring her baby home. The last note on the case was that the young mother was married to another man who adopted the little boy. There is no note on whether a clergyman was involved at any time or not, but if there was, he must have had his moments of doubt and confusion.

There was a case of a hydrocephalic baby. Josephine received her high school diploma at a maternity home the day before her daughter was born. At the graduation ceremony her mother, her two grandmothers, and her aunt were present. It was obvious to all how they doted on this capable but self-centered seventeen-year-old girl. When her baby was born and diagnosed as hydrocephalic there was concern as to how she would receive the news. The doctor explained exactly what the condition was and what the medical prospects for the baby's future were. The social worker presented the case for the possibility of adoption as gently and clearly as she could. But somewhere along the line, perhaps from the oversympathetic and sentimental women who sought to comfort her, she ran away with the idea that some loving couple was just waiting to adopt her child *because* it needed more tender loving care than other children. She refused to face the grim reality of her problem and babbled on about layettes and how her child would be more fortunate than other babies whose need was less and who would therefore receive less. There was a minister visiting this family, but it is difficult to believe he may have contributed to this unhealthy denial.

Briefly, the pastor is especially needed when there is a crisis at the birth or after the birth of the unwed mother's child.

Changing religion.   Another type of special case is the girl who wants to change her religion to that of the father of the baby for any one of several reasons. One reason may be that she is still in a state of rebellion and knows this will be a sure way to hurt her parents. Usually this becomes obvious the first time it is brought up. Neither priest, minister, nor rabbi wants any part of such a nonreligious conversion in most reported instances. Another reason is that an immature young woman who tries to involve everyone into doing things for her and tries to keep herself in the limelight in the most dramatic way possible, knows that in changing her religion, she can bring everyone front and center. The clergy of all faiths usually recognize and reject this kind of appeal. In a third kind of situation, the hopefully sentimental girl wants to change her own religion so she can bring up her baby in the father's religion. If the baby is placed for adoption, most agencies and some states insist it be in a home of the mother's religion. If she wants to circumvent this, the unwed mother changes her own affiliation before adoption. It is well to remember, however, that a change of religion when a girl is pregnant out of wedlock is not usually a religious matter at all but a symptom of the unwed mother's basic need to achieve something by this means. The pastoral counselor who recognizes this can deal with it more realistically than if he assumes his counselee's faith is at stake.

In conclusion, the following prayer is suggested for the girl whose baby is going to be or has been placed in a foster home pending adoption. The unwed mother may not ask for prayer, but few will refuse it, and they will be happy to have a copy of it to keep, yes, and to weep over.

Prayer for Baby who is going to be placed for adoption.

"O God, our heavenly Father, who has showed us through our Lord Christ that the little ones are blessed in thy kingdom, we ask that thou will richly bless . . . She is committed to thy loving care by her mother, trusting that in a good Christian home she will be so loved by both her new father and her new mother that she too may thank thee for thy loving-kindness and tender mercy in the days to come. Amen.

The following service of dedication has been used many times when an unwed mother says she would like to "do something for my baby" before it is adopted. As most pastors know, the husband and wife who have recently adopted a child are so thankful and so proud that their first thought is baptism. If the child has already been baptized, this is not possible, although special prayers of thanksgiving may be offered.

The service of dedication gives the new mother the opportunity to do that certain "something" she longs to do; it brings her experience of motherhood out of the shadows into the light of God's presence; it dignifies her relationship to her child; it brings the message of the Gospel to the occasion; it involves her in her child's future through her vows of concern and right living; and it symbolizes the placing of her child in God's loving care.

The number of letters of thanks received following a Service of Dedication is its greatest recommendation. Most of the mothers who have so presented their babies to the Lord for His blessing have wept openly during and after the Service, but have never regretted the experience no matter how much anguish they felt. No one we know of has ever changed her plans to give up her child because of it, and many have said it made the final separation easier.

The Service of Dedication[2] of the baby of the unwed mother:

SCRIPTURE

Our Lord Jesus Christ told his disciples, "Where two or three are gathered together in my name, there am I in the midst of them." (Matthew 18:20)

"Whatever you ask in my name, I will do it, that the Father may be glorified in the Son; if you ask anything in my name, I will do it." (John 14:13–14) We who profess Christ are truly his disciples.

Jesus also said, "Suffer the little children to come unto me, and forbid them not, for to such belongs the kingdom of God. Verily I say unto you, whosoever shall not receive the kingdom of God as a little child, he shall in no wise enter therein. And he took them in his arms, and blessed them, laying his hands upon them." (Mark 10:14–16)

[2] James Dalton Morrison, *Minister's Service Book for Pulpit and Parish Use* (New York: Harper & Row Publishers, 1937), p. 132.

ADDRESS TO MOTHER

Inasmuch as our Lord has taught us that the little ones are blessed in the kingdom of God, we believe it to be our duty and privilege to present them for consecration by the church, the living body of Christ on earth. In the Holy Scripture, we also read that Hannah brought the child Samuel to the House of the Lord in Shiloh, and Mary and Joseph presented the infant Jesus in the temple of Jerusalem.

No ceremony, however ancient and solemn, has power to change the character of this child or to alter . . . relationship to God. Nevertheless, you offer this child to the loving care of Almighty God, trusting in his infinite mercy that in a Christian home . . . will receive such instruction and guidance and the exemplification of right living as will determine in large measure . . . character and eternal destiny.

COVENANT

Minister: In presenting your child for dedication to God, do you affirm that you will pray without ceasing for . . . spiritual welfare and endeavor yourself to serve God in every way known to you to bring his kingdom closer?

Mother: I do.

Minister: And do you promise that in token of your belief in God's power to grant your petition you will, God being your helper, serve the interest of God's children everywhere that the least of them may grow in wisdom and stature and in favor with God and man?

Mother: I do.

(Here the minister takes the baby from the mother and goes to the altar.)

DEDICATION

Prayer: Accept, we pray thee, O God, this child . . . whom we now dedicate to thee and give us grace so to concern ourselves with whatsoever things are true and pure and lovely and of good report, following the example of our Lord Jesus Christ, that this little one may be affected by our lives.

Our Father who art in Heaven, hallowed be thy name. Thy kingdom come, thy will be done, on earth as it is in Heaven. Give us this day our daily bread; and forgive us our trespasses as we forgive those who trespass against us. Lead us not into temptation, but deliver us from evil, for thine is the kingdom and the power and the glory forever. Amen.

. . . I dedicate thee to God and to the service of his kingdom in the name of the Father and the Son and the Holy Spirit. Amen.

(Here the minister gives the baby back to the mother.)

BLESSING

The Lord bless you and keep you, and make his face to shine upon you and be gracious unto you. The Lord lift up his countenance upon you and give you peace, now and evermore. Amen.

CHAPTER TEN

CONCLUSION

In the last year or two, many local churches and at least one denomination have included the problem of out-of-wedlock pregnancy and the problems of the unwed mother in their studies of social concerns and people with special needs. Some church groups have met with social workers who worked with the unwed mother, and they have held workshops and seminars on the subject. These people know that doing volunteer work for a maternity home is not going to reduce the number of babies born out of wedlock next year. They know that persuasion from the pulpit or in the home will make little difference. They know that some new and more effective kind of punishment will not be the solution. It is as difficult to find the means for reducing the number of babies born out of wedlock as it is to find ways of preventing people from performing any other irresponsible action that brings grief to others. But this is no reason to give up the quest.

The minister strengthens his work with the unwed mother by working with all of his parishioners. It cannot be said that this one girl is in more need of help than many of the other young men and women, but her need is more obvious. By helping her, he perhaps learns to help other young women. Hopefully, he may be able to help them before they become unwed parents.

Recently, a clergyman[1] on the outskirts of a large city gave a sermon entitled, "Awake, Thou That Sleepest!" His sermon was described by his parishioners as "coping with the problem of awaken-

---

[1] The Reverend John W. Ellison, Th.D., Rector, Church of the Epiphany, Winchester, Massachusetts. March 17, 1963.

127

ing a bedroom-type community to confronting realistically the sub-
stantial increase in bedroom activities of the younger set." In his
opening remarks, he said, ". . . in the last fourteen months more
cases of promiscuity resulting in pregnancy have been brought to my
attention among the young people in this parish than in the eight
preceding years added together!" He affirmed that parents must set
limits for their children, must not be afraid of their children's wail-
ing that they are harsh and unfair, and that not all the whims of
youth must be served. He pointed out that many young people
chafe at restrictions and complain, "But everybody else is allowed to
do it." The minister concluded, "Somebody must begin by taking
a public stand to which other parents can repair." In closing he
offered his own services. "If any parents feel that the above points
are a good beginning for standards in this community, let them send
me their names and addresses. I will compile the names and addresses, sending each one a list of the others so that he will know
which other parents in the community are ready and willing to take
a stand." Bringing out of the shadows the behavior of the young
people and their parents' reactions to it is a positive and immediate
step that helps meet the problem of out-of-wedlock pregnancy.

As already mentioned, some church study groups have devoted
time to this subject. The mothers of young children have shown the
most personal interest, probably because they feel that they have so
much at stake. At one meeting, questions of one group of mothers
were collected before the program began and were answered by the
speaker after his talk. These questions asked on this particular occasion indicate previous serious thought and reflect the subjective
nature of the mothers' concern. They wanted to know:

What is the Christian view of the unwed mother?
What are the attitudes of the girls? Do they have a sense of guilt or
remorse?
What do you consider is the major reason that teen-agers engage in
premarital sexual relations?
What earlier influences, or lack of them, do these girls feel caused
them to make the mistake they did?
What happens to the basically good girls after they give up their babies
and return to society?

What are the chances for the unwed mother to lead a normal life after the birth of her child?

In addition to giving our children guidance, how can we help prevent such a thing from happening to them?

Can you give us any advice that might help us to raise our daughters? Do you think the way a mother dresses and accepts her own duties makes a difference?

A minister might use questions similar to these as a basis for a discussion of the problem of the unwed mother with members of his parish. Hopefully, such a positive effort on the part of parishioners and pastor together will lead to both the thoughtful acceptance of the girl who has been an unwed mother and at the same time be a significant step toward preventing the same thing from happening to other young women in the community.

Even though earnest groups of laymen, young mothers, older women, and youth fellowships are all concerned with checking the increase of out-of-wedlock pregnancy in the United States today, nothing significant can be done until the family as a unit begins to examine itself and face its responsibilities. There is much talk about broken homes; they are more dramatic, but less corrosive to society, than the fragmented families that live at the same address. It is more important for members of the family to be able to communicate with each other and understand each other, than it is for a family of strangers to be seen together at every social function. How many of our churches are working toward the goal of helping their church families become families at home? It is as senseless for people to think that family relationships are of no concern to the church as it is for them to suppose that personal ethics are unrelated to the Christian fellowship.

The existence of out-of-wedlock pregnancies is evidence that our young people's concept of the family has been distorted. We suggest that people in the parish who are concerned about this aspect of Christian life may be persuaded to gather for a study that begins at the center of Christian life, that is, their own family. It is in the family context that character is built, religion is nurtured, and value systems are acquired. The religious teachings and moral standards of the Church may prove unequal to the task of redeeming those whom their family has ignored. Only as the Church becomes representative of the Incarnation, only as the people who are the Church act in the spirit of Christ, will the Church have a positive influence on both the problem of the out-of-wedlock pregnancy and the problems of the unwed mother.

BIBLIOGRAPHY

BOOKS

ACKERMAN, NATHAN W., *The Psychodynamics of Family Life; Diagnosis and Treatment of Family Relationships.* New York: Basic Books, Inc., 1958. Ch. 21.

BAINTON, ROLAND H., *What Christianity Says About Sex, Love and Marriage.* Reflection Book. New York: Association Press, 1957.

COLE, WILLIAM GRAHAM, *Sex and Love in the Bible.* New York: Association Press, 1959.

DENTON, WALLACE, *What's Happening to Our Families?* Philadelphia: The Westminster Press, 1963.

DEUTSCH, HELENE, *The Psychology of Women: A Psychoanalytic Interpretation,* Vol. II. New York: Grune & Stratton, Inc., 1945. Ch. 10.

DUVALL, EVELYN M., and SYLVANUS M., *Sense and Nonsense About Sex.* A Teen-Age Reflection Book. New York: Association Press, 1962.

HARDING, M. ESTHER, *The Way of All Women.* New York: Longmans, Green and Co., Inc., 1933.

HILTNER, SEWARD, *Sex and the Christian Life.* Reflection Book. New York: Association Press, 1957.

JOSLIN, G. STANLEY, *The Minister's Law Handbook.* Manhasset, N.Y.: Channel Press, 1962. pp. 27–32, 107–111.

MAY, ROLLO, *The Meaning of Anxiety.* New York: Ronald Press, 1950.

PARSONS, TALCOTT, "A Sociologist's View." Reprinted from *Values and Ideals of American Youth,* ed. Eli Ginzberg. New York: Columbia University Press, 1961. pp. 271–287.

THIELICKE, HELMUT, *The Ethics of Sex.* New York, Harper and Row, 1963.

VINCENT, CLARK E., *Unmarried Mothers.* New York, The Free Press of Glencoe, Inc., 1961.

VINCENT, CLARK E., ed., *Premarital Sex Relations: The Facts and the Counselor's Role in Relation to the Facts. A Symposium in Readings in Marriage Counseling.* New York, Thomas Y. Crowell, Co., 1957.

YOUNG, LEONTINE R., *Out of Wedlock.* New York: McGraw-Hill Book Co., Inc., 1954.

PERIODICALS

ADAMS, HANNAH M., and GALLAGHER, URSULA M., "Some Facts and Observations about Illegitimacy," *Children* (March–April, 1963), pp. 43–48.

BERNSTEIN, ROSE, "Are We Still Stereotyping the Unmarried Mother?" *Social Work* (July, 1960), pp. 22–28.

———, "Gaps in Services to Unmarried Mothers," *Children* (March–April, 1963), pp. 49–54.

BOOLE, LUCILE G., "The Hospital and Unmarried Mothers," *Children* (Nov.–Dec., 1956), pp. 208–212.

CLOTHIER, FLORENCE, "Psychological Implications of Unmarried Parenthood," *American Journal of Orthopsychiatry* (July, 1945), pp. 531–549.

CORNER, GEORGE M., "Science and Sex Ethics," *Saturday Evening Post* (Oct. 10, 1959), pp. 20, 61–63.

CURTIS, HESTER B., and DE RONGÉ, ALBERTA, "Medical and Social Care for Unmarried Mothers," *Children* (Sept.–Oct., 1957), pp. 174–180.

FROMER, ANNE, "'Nice Girls' Are Dangerous," *Coronet* (Sept., 1954), pp. 77–82.

GALLAGHER, URSULA M., "Interprofessional Teamwork to Safeguard Adoptions," *Children* (May–June, 1951), pp. 101–104.

GARLAND, PATRICIA, "The Community's Part in Preventing Illegitimacy," *Children* (March–April, 1963), pp. 71–75.

GRAY, PAUL H., "Conscience, Guilt and the Unwed Mother," *The Journal of Pastoral Care* (Fall, 1951), pp. 164–170.

HERTZ, HILDA, and LITTLE, SUE WARREN, "Unmarried Negro Mothers in a Southern Urban Community," *Social Forces* (Oct., 1944), pp. 73–79.

HERZOG, ELIZABETH, "Unmarried Mothers: Some Questions to Be Answered and Some Answers to Be Questioned," *Child Welfare* (Oct., 1962), pp. 339–350.

"ILLEGITIMACY AND DEPENDENCY," U.S. Dept. of Health, Education and Welfare, Washington, D.C., *Indicators*, Sept. 1963.

KATZ, SANFORD N., "Legal Protections for the Unmarried Mother and Her Child," *Children* (March–April, 1963), pp. 55–59.

LATIMER, RUTH, and STARTSMAN, FLORENCE, "The Role of the Maternity Home Social Worker in the Prevention of Illegitimacy," *Mental Hygiene* (July, 1963), pp. 470–476.

LEE, ROBERT, "Delinquent Youth in Normless Time," *The Christian Century* (Dec. 5, 1962), pp. 1475–1478.

LEVY, DOROTHY, "A Follow-up Study of Unmarried Mothers," *Social Casework* (Jan., 1955), pp. 27–33.

MAY, ROLLO, "Where Do Religion and Psychotherapy Meet?" *United Church Herald* (March 12, 1959), pp. 14–15, 28.

MEAD, MARGARET, "The Changing American Family," *Children* (Sept.–Oct., 1963), pp. 173–174.

MEIER, ELIZABETH G., "Independent Adoptions—Ten Years Later," *Children* (Nov.–Dec., 1963), pp. 230–232.

PANNOR, REUBEN, "Casework Service for Unmarried Fathers," *Children* (March–April, 1963), pp. 65–70.

PRIESTLEY, J. B., "Eroticism, Sex and Love," *Saturday Evening Post* (April 27, 1963), pp. 10, 14.

REIDER, NORMAN, "The Unmarried Father," *American Journal of Orthopsychiatry* (April, 1948), pp. 230–237.

SHUPP, CLEO, "Little Girls Are Sexy Too Soon," *Saturday Evening Post* (June 29–July 6, 1963), pp. 12, 16.

"UNMARRIED PARENTS: What Is and Is Not Being Done for Them and About Them," *Children* (March–April, 1963). This is the theme of the entire issue.

VINCENT, CLARK E., "Illegitimacy and Value Dilemmas," *Christian Century* (June 19, 1963), pp. 801–804.

YOUNG, LEONTINE, "Why Does a Girl Become an Unmarried Mother?" *Pastoral Psychology* (April, 1958), pp. 42–49.

PAPERS And PAMPHLETS

ALPENFELS, ESTHER J., "Values, Goals of Youth in Our Culture; Their Impact on the Problem of Illegitimacy Among Adolescents" (1962). Paper delivered at the National Conference on Social Welfare.

AMERICAN INSTITUTE OF FAMILY RELATIONS, 5287 Sunset Boulevard, Los Angeles 27, California. Publishes many pamphlets and booklets useful to pastor, parent and young person, for personal help or group study. List available.

CHILD WELFARE LEAGUE OF AMERICA, INC., 345 E. 46 St., New York 17, N.Y., "Standards for Services to Unmarried Parents" (1960).

——, "Brief and Intensive Casework with Unmarried Mothers" (April, 1963).

GREENLEIGH ASSOCIATES, INC., 437 Fifth Ave., New York, N.Y. "Facts, Fallacies and Future: A Study in Aid to Dependent Children Program, Cook County, Illinois" (1960).

NATIONAL ASSOCIATION OF SERVICES TO UNMARRIED PARENTS, 120 Grand St., White Plains, New York. "Directory of Maternity Homes." May be purchased.

NATIONAL STUDY SERVICE, "Illegitimacy and Adoption in Maine" (1963). Report of a study made for the Maine Committee on Children and Youth.

SALVATION ARMY, "Services to Unmarried Parents and Their Children" (Feb., 1962). Lists maternity homes and hospitals. Handbook of information.

U.S. DEPARTMENT OF HEALTH, EDUCATION AND WELFARE, CHILDREN'S BUREAU, Washington, D.C.: U.S. Government Printing Office:

French, T. M., "The Importance of the First Interview with the Unwed Mothers" (1952).

Gallagher, Ursula M., "The Unmarried Mother Situation in the United States Today" (1959).

Morlock, Maude, "Fathers of Children Born Out of Wedlock" (1939).

"Social Services for Unmarried Mothers and Their Children Provided Through Public and Voluntary Child Welfare Agencies," Report No. 12 (1962).

"The Unmarried Father" (1940).

INDEX

INDEX